LEADERSHIP

FOR

TOMORROW'S

SCHOOLS

JERRY L. PATTERSON

Association for Supervision and Curriculum Development

Association for Supervision and Curriculum Development
1250 N. Pitt St., Alexandria, VA 22314.
Telephone: (703) 549-9110. Fax: (703) 549-3891 or 836-7921.

ASCD publications present a variety of viewpoints. The views expressed or implied
in this publication should not be interpreted as official positions of the Association.

Printed in the United States of America.

Ronald S. Brandt, *Executive Editor*
Nancy Modrak, *Managing Editor, Books and Editorial Services*
Julie Houtz, *Senior Associate Editor*
Jennifer Beun, *Assistant Editor*
Gary Bloom, *Manager, Design and Production Services*
Stephanie Kenworthy, *Asst. Mgr., Design and Production Services*
Karen Monaco, *Senior Graphic Designer*
Valerie Sprague, *Typesetting Specialist*

ASCD Stock No.: 611-93121
Price: $11.95
ISBN: 0-87120-209-3

Library of Congress Cataloging-in-Publication Data

Patterson, Jerry L., 1944–
    Leadership for tomorrow's schools / Jerry L. Patterson.
        p.   cm.
    Includes bibliographical references (p.   ) and index.
    ISBN 0-87120-209-3 : $11.95
    1. Educational leadership—Wisconsin—Appleton—Case studies.
    2. School management and organization—Wisconsin—Appleton—Case studies.
    3. Decision-making—Wisconsin—Appleton—Case studies. 4. Organizational
    behavior—Wisconsin—Appleton—Case studies.
    I. Title.
    LB2831.824.W6P38   1992
    371.2′07—dc20   93-19133
                                                                       CIP

LEADERSHIP

FOR TOMORROW'S

SCHOOLS

FOREWORD

Most of us are all too familiar with the hierarchical structure that places leaders at the apex of a pyramid of employees, poised to use their superior knowledge and experience to direct and control the workings of an entire organization. Organizations worldwide, including schools, have been built on this concept of the leader directing others to fulfill a vision conceived and designed by that leader. In *Leadership for Tomorrow's Schools*, Jerry Patterson challenges this paradigm and suggests that the eye at the top of the pyramid is often blind to the realities of the workplace. Patterson observes that we are virtual slaves to a system that just doesn't work in today's complex and rapidly changing world.

In Patterson's plan for liberating the organization, leadership is fluid, changing with time to meet emerging needs. The distinctive feature of this new approach is its participatory framework; however, it is by no means mere participative management, for it involves much more than the coordination of people and resources. It involves creating a vision of a "preferred future" and developing "a shared commitment to core values" that will, by their very nature, change how people work together. In tomorrow's organization, people will share the responsibilities and rewards of leadership and work together to improve the "system" of which they are all a part.

Leaders struggling to redefine their schools and establish a viable course of action for the 21st century will find this book a valuable resource, potent with practical strategies for liberating their organization. I found it a particularly appropriate book for ASCD members because it directly addresses our mission of "developing leadership for quality in education for all students." We in the profession would do well to follow Jerry Patterson's guidelines and reexamine the fundamental values we bring to the workplace. We owe it to ourselves and the students we serve to cast off outdated concepts of leadership and move into the future with "passion and confidence," embracing a leadership stance that enables educators and students alike to reach their potential.

—BARBARA TALBERT JACKSON
ASCD President, 1992–93

PREFACE

Just when we think we understand how this thing called leadership works, somebody changes the rules on us. *Leadership for Tomorrow's Schools* does indeed change the rules.

I didn't set out to change the rules. I set out on a journey trying to make sense of what leading will look like in the future. I soon realized that leading tomorrow is not simply a more enlightened version of leading today. In fact, it may be the opposite of how we lead in today's organization.

I also set out to describe leadership from a superintendent's perspective. As a friend once told me, "Where you stand depends on where you sit." Where I stand on the issue of leadership is heavily influenced by the seat I occupy as superintendent of schools. This book brings together the collective wisdom of researchers and theorists such as Peter Senge and Stephen Covey and meshes it with the collective experience of colleagues I've had the good fortune to work with in the real world of schools and school districts.

The product is a powerful and radical departure from how most of us were taught to lead. You will learn about the values and principles tomorrow's leaders will live by, the conflicts they will face, and the outcomes they will expect. By book's end, I expect you will see yourself as one of tomorrow's leaders.

—JERRY PATTERSON

1

EXCHANGING

TODAY'S VALUES FOR

TOMORROW'S VALUES

Imagine you are the long-standing, successful coach of a basketball team. Tonight your team is playing for the league championship. When the players walk onto the floor for warm-ups, the head official calls you aside and informs you of the following rule changes:

- When a team gets the ball, it determines how many points its next shot counts.
- Double dribbling is okay. Even triple dribbling will be allowed.
- Coaches may have as many players on the floor at one time as they choose.
- The team playing defense may adjust the height of the basket anytime they choose.
- The game ends when the officials say it ends.

As a coach, how would you react to these rule changes? Even a great coach might be somewhat disoriented by them, because they change the game in significant ways. The rules for success have been redefined. Some coaches might refuse to play by the new rules. Others would do their best to adapt to them.

In a similar way, the rules for leadership in American business, education, and industry are also changing. In fact, I believe the United States is on the brink of a fundamentally different framework for describing and understanding leadership in all of our major institutions. In a world turned upside down by technology, major shifts in political power, and a rapidly emerging global economy, we must try to better understand the shift that is taking place in our thinking about leadership.

THE SHIFTING DEFINITIONS OF LEADERSHIP

For most of us, leadership is an elusive concept. Definitions vary from person to person, from organization to organization, and from one year to the next. We all know we need it, but we're not quite sure exactly what it is that we need. Thus, in our eagerness to establish leadership, we are willing to seize anything that seems remotely related to our foggy notions of what leaders should provide. In most cases, the result has been that we have one of two other things masquerading as leadership: bossing or managing.

BOSSING

For the past seventy-five years, the idea of leadership has reflected the industrial model of governing organizations. More specifically, despite voices arguing to the contrary, leadership has consistently been characterized by the central values of *power* and *control*. Organizations have been conceived, constructed, and evaluated on the premise that leaders are responsible for directing and controlling the organization. Through the pyramid of the hierarchical structure, the people at the top direct the people in the middle to tell the people at the bottom what to do. All employees do—or pretend to do—what they are told. In this model, successful leaders exercise formal authority to exert real power to make things happen as they have planned. In other words, they spend their days bossing.

Today's leaders most likely got where they are by conforming to these unwritten but powerful rules for successful leadership. Unlike the rules for basketball, organizational rules typically grow out of cherished beliefs about what is important and why. This book challenges most of the traditional beliefs about leadership. A major thesis of this book is that these beliefs or values don't describe the essence of leading at all. They describe bossing.

MANAGING

Managing is another concept often confused with leadership. Managing is the act of coordinating people and resources to efficiently produce goods or services in an organization. Managing is critical to the success of an organization and is performed at all levels of the organization. Managing is even part of what leaders do. But managing is not the same as leading.

LEADING

If bossing is not leading, and if managing is not leading, then what are we talking about here? In the organization of tomorrow, leading is defined as *the process of influencing others to achieve mutually agreed upon purposes for the organization.* So far, this probably sounds to you like just another dry, academic definition with no basis in reality. If we examine this definition more closely, however, we may see it come to life.

The first piece of this definition is the notion of leadership as a process. This idea precludes the traditional "Great Person Theory," which holds that leaders are leaders because they possess admirable characteristics or traits. In tomorrow's organization, however, a person who is, say, visionary, charismatic, organized, and a good listener is not necessarily going to be a successful leader.

The idea of influencing others is the second piece of this definition of leadership. Influencing implies a relationship among people. The emphasis shifts away from the individual and toward the interaction patterns among individuals. Although leading may involve persuasion, it does not involve coercion or bossing. Moreover, the direction and amount of influence are determined not by a person's place on the organizational chart, but by the expertise a person brings to the issue at hand.

The third piece of this definition of leadership is "to achieve mutually agreed upon purposes for the organization." In other words, the organization's goals are supported by all people involved, and these people in turn support those who are, at that particular time, leading them toward the goals. As time passes, however, leaders may become followers, and followers may become leaders. Roles are not fixed.

Taken together, these three components of the concept of leadership produce a dynamic greater than the sum of the parts. Tomorrow's leaders will be vastly different from today's leaders. Granted, anyone can call what he or she is doing leading. Someone may argue that he is the leader of a gang. Someone else may claim that she is the leader of a military commando unit. In both cases, they are in charge and people are expected to follow their orders. But by tomorrow's standards, they are not leaders.

CHANGING THE RULES

At the beginning of this chapter, I described a fictitious set of rule changes for basketball that would alter the way people play the game. Now let's consider some real-life value changes for organizations that will alter the way people lead organizations. We're going to focus our discussion on the concept of openness. "Why openness?" you might ask. Well, imagine you work within a box. The dimensions of this box define how freely you can move about. In other words, they define the "openness" of the organization in which you work. The dimensions themselves are determined by the organization's values, so we are going to consider the degree of openness in today's organization based on the prevailing value structure and then contrast this level of openness with the level of openness in tomorrow's organization operating under a different value structure. For the purposes of our discussion, we will consider openness as it relates to five important areas: participation, diversity, conflict, reflection, and mistakes.

Leaders often run headlong into the natural limits imposed by the values defining today's organization. As leaders try to open up their organization by embracing values such as participation, diversity, and reflection, they face a constant tension resulting from the conflict between these values and the current values used to judge successful leadership. As we see later in this book, the more leaders try to pull away from today's values, the greater the force to conform to them. Eventually, leaders are pushed up against the walls of the box. If they want room to maneuver, they must leap into a different box—that is, into a disorienting new world of leadership governed by new values.

Breaking out of the old box is risky business for leaders. To do so, they must throw away values based on personal power and control and accept new values based on the power of the organization as a whole and the commitment to core values. When faced with the prospect of change, many leaders are tempted to retreat to the safety of the familiar box, to the old values they have known so well. Those who make the leap into the new box, however, usually find the risk was well worth taking.

CONTRASTING TODAY'S AND TOMORROW'S VALUES

Today's organizational values significantly limit openness. We can see how by contrasting today's and tomorrow's values concerning our five key value areas.

VALUE 1: OPENNESS TO PARTICIPATION

Today's Value:	Our organization values employees listening to the organization's leaders and doing what the leaders tell them to do.
Tomorrow's Value:	Our organization values employees actively participating in any discussion or decision affecting them.

Most leaders today believe one of the most important aspects of a strong organization is having everything "under control." How they reach a decision is far less important than the substance of the decision, for in their mind, their job is to make good decisions. They also believe they are responsible for controlling what happens in the organization. This feeling of responsibility usually causes today's leaders to discount the ideas of other employees. In fact, leaders who "allow" all employees to participate in decision making are often considered weak by other leaders. Today's leaders believe that someone has to be in charge and say, "Thank you for the comments, but we have to move on. I'll let you know what I have decided." Although they may allow employees to have a voice in some matters, they usually reserve the important decisions for themselves because they have learned to value power and control.

Even enlightened leaders are constrained by the walls of today's box. Before they can institute real change, they must change their values—that is, they must change boxes. In this case, they must turn their back on the value of exercising personal authority over events and people to get the right decisions made and, instead, embrace the idea of overseeing the development and implementation of a set of core values that will drive decision making by all employees.

As values change, so do the measures of organizational strengths and weaknesses. In this case, they are reversed. Based on tomorrow's value, a strong organization is characterized by employees throughout the organization participating in virtually all decisions (except, perhaps, personnel issues and overarching budget targets). Leaders in tomorrow's organization want, even expect, employee participation. When active participation becomes a core value, a weak organization is characterized by a top-down approach that requires employees to listen to the leaders and to do what they are told.

To better understand how our attitude toward participation affects decision making, let's look at an example. Suppose several school employees question the practice of granting senior administrators the reserved parking spaces closest to the front door of the building. Operating under today's value concerning participation, the superintendent invites the questioners to her office and explains that reserved parking spaces have been a perk for senior administrators for as long as anyone can remember. This special treatment gives others something to aim for. The superintendent genuinely thanks the employees for raising the question and providing the chance for explanation. Power and control are at the heart of this interaction. The boss has simply told the employees why the decision was made.

In tomorrow's organization, this scenario would play out differently, because tomorrow's organization values employee participation; it expects and encourages employees to challenge the practices of the organization, especially if the practices seem inconsistent with the organization's expressed values. In this case, participation might translate to a committee of employees examining the consistency between values and practices related to reserved parking spaces, and then presenting recommendations for criteria to be applied equally to all employees who would like parking spaces. These criteria will determine who, if anyone, should regularly occupy the most coveted parking spaces.

Active participation spells trouble if leaders worry about controlling the outcomes. Participation becomes a true value only when we believe that participation produces a collective wisdom that surpasses any individual's knowledge of an issue. "We are smarter than me" must become a prevailing belief in the organization. How might this belief translate into action? Well, suppose five people come to a meeting, each with a different proposal for controlling health-care costs in our organization. Instead of debating each of the five proposals and choosing the best one, our leader requests that we list on chart paper the strongest feature of each. We then build a new proposal capitalizing on our individual thoughts. This new proposal is the result of group consensus and will undoubtedly be stronger than any of the individual proposals.

It's important to emphasize that tomorrow's organization values active participation by *all* employees. Organizations that embrace the idea of participation typically begin with the professional employees. Unfortunately, participation usually stops there, even though the organization has identified employee participation as a core value. By definition, however, a core value is one that applies to everyone. The secretary, custodian, and other employees deserve the same invitation to participate openly in discussions that touch their work lives. That invitation signals to employees that each person is an equally valued member of the organization.

Ensuring that everyone has the opportunity to participate will almost certainly require that decision making take more time. In most organizations, time is already a precious commodity; however, tomorrow's leaders believe that participation by all employees is a higher organizational value than the practical question of the time necessary to make the value come alive.

VALUE 2: OPENNESS TO DIVERSITY

Today's Value: Our organization values employees falling in line with the overall organizational direction.

Tomorrow's Value: Our organization values diversity in perspectives leading to a deeper understanding of organizational reality and an enriched knowledge base for decision making.

As much as leaders may want to honor diversity, success in today's organization is measured by conformity. Leaders can't waste energy trying to corral strays. They are so pressed to make timely, cost-effective decisions that they grow impatient with dissenters. Maverick voices, they believe, weaken the organization's team spirit and lead to a breakdown in organizational loyalty, which today is measured by the degree to which employees think and act as they are told to by those in charge. In fact, today's leaders believe a sure sign of organizational weakness is employees who feel compelled to express views that conflict with organization directives. Although they may say that different viewpoints are important, they don't want employees to step outside the paths already determined by the organization.

The full meaning of openness would be incomplete without the element of openness to diverse opinions. In tomorrow's organization, this value becomes extremely important as leaders discover the power of having a broad and deep picture of organizational reality, an understanding of what is happening throughout the organization. Leaders like to believe they have an accurate view of the organization, but their view is necessarily limited. They cannot possibly perceive all that is happening in every nook and cranny of the organization, for organizational reality is complex and subjective. It is, in fact, a product of the different circumstances and points of view of each employee.

To illustrate, imagine you and I are among the seven senior administrators who are meeting to discuss the future of decentralization in our organization. As the ranking administrator for business and data processing, you describe your unit's view of the need for decentralization. The reality, from where you sit, is that centralization is more efficient and more effective for achieving the major organizational objectives in your division. The reality is documented in your staff's twenty-page position paper supporting the cost-effectiveness of maintaining centralization. I counter your arguments from the perspective of the senior administrator responsible for quality service to our stakeholders. I demonstrate through numerous examples that we need to move decision making closer to those responsible for providing quality service. The reality, from where I sit, is that those in the field can most effectively and efficiently determine areas for improving service. Each of these realities is a piece of the bigger organizational reality. Both are valid and important, because together they help us see the organization in more comprehensive and realistic terms.

In tomorrow's organization, the signs of strength and weakness are the opposite of those in today's organization. Diversity is valued and celebrated. Employees are encouraged to express their opinions—even when they go against the prevailing view. Tomorrow's organization frowns on practices that force employees to automatically fall in line with the stated organizational direction. All of us recognize that only by involving everyone can we gain the rich knowledge and understanding necessary to see the total organizational picture.

VALUE 3: OPENNESS TO CONFLICT

Today's Value:	Our organization values employees communicating a climate of group harmony and happiness.
Tomorrow's Value:	Our organization values employees resolving conflict in a healthy way that leads to stronger solutions for complex issues.

Today, more than ever, conflict between individuals seems inevitable. The rapid pace of change and the constant bombardment of new information work together to keep people stirred up. Our typical response to conflict is to ignore it, hoping it will disappear by itself. Left alone, however, conflict rarely disappears; instead, it grows and festers, feeding our aversion to it.

Though today's leaders may acknowledge that employees need to let off steam every once in a while, they have been taught that group conflict and tension are bad. These conditions mean things aren't going smoothly in the organization and someone—usually the leader—has to straighten them out. But today's leaders don't like to deal with conflict, so they take steps to prevent it from ever occurring. The message employees receive is usually loud and clear: if you are unhappy about the way this organization is run, you are a disloyal employee; you are siphoning off energy and detracting from our image of one big happy family working in harmony; you are a drag on the organization.

When conflict does bubble to the surface, leaders usually advise that disputes between individuals are best handled privately, outside the meeting room. Although they realize they can't ignore disagreements over organizational issues, they do their best to keep them from disrupting their meeting agendas because they believe that arguments rarely lead to a productive conclusion. As a result, conflict arising in meetings is almost always moved to another time and place so the meeting can continue "on track." Obviously, today's leaders view conflict and argument as a weakness in the fundamental structure of the organization.

Tomorrow's leaders, however, embrace conflict. By valuing the energy of dissent, they let people inside and outside the organization know where they stand: honest conflict in a safe environment provides the seeds for rich solutions to organizational issues.

Consider this scenario: In a department meeting, you and I disagree about the most effective strategy for controlling costs in our department. You argue that we need to impose a 10 percent reduction across all functions, spreading the burden equally. I contend that we need to determine our priority areas, fund them fully, and make our cuts more substantially (up to 75 percent) in less important areas. The debate becomes heated, and colleagues start taking sides. The leader of the meeting responds by refocusing the debate on what we are trying to accomplish, not on who wins or loses this argument. Ultimately, our heated dialogue leads us to a group consensus that cost reductions should be fair; fairness, however, should not necessarily be defined as equal cuts in all areas. The group also concludes that priority areas should be given special attention; the areas we finally agree are priorities, however, turn out to be different from those I had in mind. In this meeting, the spark of conflict created energy that led to a group decision stronger than any individual recommendation put forth during the conflict.

Conflict creates tension. Tension flags a gap between what is and what ought to be. Leaders can use tension creatively by capitalizing on the energy of dissent and forcing us to critically examine our strongly held positions or beliefs. In the organization of tomorrow, today's organizational strength becomes tomorrow's weakness. Something is wrong inside the organization if employees seem to always be in harmony. On the other hand, the organization is on the right track if employees feel free to engage in heated debate, acknowledge the conflict, then develop organizational strategies to resolve their differences in a healthy way. When conflict is handled constructively in a safe environment, both the individual and the organization become stronger, though not always without some measure of pain.

VALUE 4: OPENNESS TO REFLECTION

Today's Value:	Our organization values employees conveying a climate of decisiveness. Firm decisions are made and implemented without looking back.
Tomorrow's Value:	Our organization values employees reflecting on their own and others' thinking in order to achieve better organizational decisions.

In today's organization, leaders realize the organization can't continue to do the same things in the same way or they will continue to get the same results. Time to reflect on the old ways of working can help to break this pattern, yet taking time to reflect forces leaders to run the risk of failing to pull their train into the station precisely on time. And today's leaders have been taught that organizations suffer major penalties for delays. This mentality discourages employees from pausing to reflect on what they're doing and why they're doing it.

When leaders find themselves approaching the outer limits of reflection in today's box, they often retreat swiftly. They know that if they step outside the box, they will be faced with new and unfamiliar values. At least in today's box, they say, they know how their success will be judged. Besides, if leaders turn people loose to question, second-guess others, or change their mind, they could end up taking mental trips to destinations unknown. They might even find themselves stuck with a set of values, assumptions, and ways of doing business that have no place in their vision for the organization. A clear sign of weakness in today's organization is an environment where everything is up for grabs, where people question the way things are done. Today's leaders believe they have a responsibility to make sure that reflection, if it occurs, doesn't deter them from achieving the vision they have set for the organization. Reflection may have its place, as long as it is understood to be secondary to making firm decisions without looking back.

Earlier I suggested that "we are smarter than me." When it comes to reflection, tomorrow's leaders understand the power generated by group-think—that is, thinking governed by particular values. In tomorrow's organization, groupthink does not translate into group think-alike. Instead, it means that powerful solutions occur when several things happen:

1. *Leaders create an environment of safety, so all employees can freely express their thoughts without fear of intimidation or recrimination.* Leaders have an ethical obligation to make sure there is a safety net under every person who becomes vulnerable in the course of questioning, challenging, and outright criticizing their own or others' thinking. In other words, reflecting out loud is risky business in front of a group. Most of us refuse to do it because we see nothing to catch us if we stumble.

2. *We learn to separate the person from the issue.* Employees need to know that the organization supports collegial disagreement about ideas, not personal attacks against individuals. It's only human to sometimes become defensive at what appears to be an attack on the quality of our assumptions or conclusions. In a collegial atmosphere, however, we can publicly ac-knowledge, "Yes, I am defensive, and it's okay to be that way occasionally." This public acknowledgement frees employees to be vulnerable within the group. Becoming vulnerable helps us see each other as people who laugh, cry, worry, and celebrate. It makes us real, not just symbols on the organ-izational chart. However, once I make myself vulnerable and you attack *me* rather than the *issue*, I retreat and will not engage in reflective thinking again with you around.

3. *Individuals develop the capacity to publicly challenge their own thinking, even if it reveals some uncertainty on their part.* In today's box, firm decisions and personal certainty are prized. In tomorrow's box, these characteristics become weaknesses, inhibiting the ability of the organization to grow through reflection. Through heavy doses of training and modeling appro-priate behavior, leaders need to nurture a reflective environment, one characterized by people suspending premature judgments, making them-selves vulnerable through questioning their own and other's thinking, and committing themselves as a group to the belief that through reflective thought *we* indeed will prove to be smarter than *me*.

VALUE 5: OPENNESS TO MISTAKES

Today's Value: Our organization values employees concentrating on making no mistakes and working as efficiently as possible.

Tomorrow's Value: Our organization values employees acknowledging mistakes and learning from them.

We have been taught since infancy to avoid making mistakes. All our lives, we have been punished for doing things wrong and rewarded for doing things right. In most cases, it's no different where we work. The well-worn cliché "Nobody's perfect" offers little guidance about organizational tolerance for mistakes. We hear repeatedly how American workers, in contrast to workers in other countries, take more time to produce products inferior to those of many other countries. "Nobody's perfect" is rapidly being replaced by "Get it right the first time," and "Strive for zero defects." These messages tend to reinforce our belief that the real measure of an employee is his contribution to a system of zero defects and efficiency. The real message is clear: "Get it right the first time—or else!" A sure sign of weakness in today's organization is employees who talk openly about their mistakes and don't keep efficiency uppermost in their mind.

In tomorrow's organization, genuine openness to mistakes calls for a wholesale shift in thinking about the meaning of mistakes. The new value begins with the attitude that I could be wrong and you could be right. Imagine the reaction to such a statement under today's model: If I am wrong, then I can't possibly have as much to contribute as you, the right one. In tomorrow's organization, we will see things differently. If I am wrong and you are right, then both the organization and I stand to learn a great deal, especially once we understand *why* your perspective appears to be the right one.

Tomorrow's leaders also encourage employees to entertain the possibility that I could be right and you could be right—or both of us could be wrong. So often we get caught up in either-or thinking because most of us were taught that there is one best answer to every question, and we were rewarded for finding that answer. In tomorrow's organization, we will find that some questions just don't have one best answer. We will discover that many right answers are possible, even necessary, in solving complex problems.

Although we certainly won't encourage people to make mistakes in tomorrow's organization, we will encourage people to acknowledge the mistakes they do make and apply what they have learned from their mistakes to strengthen the organization and themselves. Admitting mistakes makes us more humble, but tomorrow's leaders will value humility. Admitting mistakes exposes our limitations, but tomorrow's leaders will publicly expose their own limitations, signaling to the organization that all of us are human, all subject to weaknesses.

By shedding the image of Mr. or Ms. Right, employees in tomorrow's organization will be free to receive authentic feedback about their performance, even if the feedback points to mistakes made. In the past, we were afraid to admit our mistakes. The old values concerning mistakes forced us to conceal what we discovered about our mistakes so we didn't lose face. Consequently, we piled up mistakes that eventually led to serious problems. Tomorrow, we will receive feedback that challenges our beliefs and grow from the experience.

■　■　■

In this chapter, I have proposed a framework for thinking about organizations. This framework is not an extension of our current way of conducting business. It is a fundamentally different approach to opening up the organization in five areas: participation, diversity, conflict, reflection, and mistakes. This is not only a new way of doing business, but a risky way of doing business and a basis for skepticism from today's leaders. In fact, at this stage in the book, skepticism may be the norm for readers. In the next chapter, I acknowledge that skepticism is okay and offer support to help the skeptics move ahead.

2

Helping Skeptics Overcome Their Doubts

Many people are skeptical of the need for substantial change. "Do we really have to change the rules?" they ask. Of course we don't have to change the rules. There are plenty of reasons to leave everything alone. Most of them, however, can be boiled down into two groups, them and me.

It's Their Fault! They Won't Let Me Do It!

When I say, "They won't let me do it!" I communicate a lot more than I realize. By using the word "they," I align everybody else against me. By using the words "won't let," I give other people control over me. And by using the words "me do it," I signal that I am performing solo. One short sentence reveals many assumptions.

Identifying Who "They" Are

"They" are many different groups who have, or should have, a voice in how our organization does business. To liberate the organization, leaders must get all stakeholders on board. In most schools, there are three primary groups of stakeholders.

Employees. Employees are one group of stakeholders who have justifiable reasons to resist the kind of wholesale change we're talking about here. For one, they have most likely already had to change in ways they don't support. In recent years, many organizations have bombarded their employees with so many newfangled, short-lived ideas for improvement that it's no wonder employees respond to new ideas with, "This, too, shall pass."

Employees have other, equally valid reasons for rejecting change: time, money, energy, motivation, personal return on investment. With all of these disincentives for contemplating significant change, why continue this dialogue about changing values? Because we are talking about significant changes that will improve employees' lives, not cosmetic changes designed to mask the scars left by the organization's previous ways of doing business. We are talking about major surgery that will improve the way all of us think, feel, and act on the job—and most likely off the job too.

Leaders cannot assume, however, that they know how employees will think and feel about tomorrow's values. They cannot institute something from on high, for doing so would violate the spirit of tomorrow's values. Instead, they must live those values and involve employees in creating their own core values. A good way to begin is to pose questions like those in Figure 2.1. The answers can provide the foundation on which to build a set of organizational values related to the five aspects of openness discussed earlier.

Unions. Employees aren't the only "they" group out there. In many organizations, union leaders are a significant group of stakeholders. Although employees are members of the union, the interests of individual employees sometimes differ from the interests of the union. In this case, for instance, the idea of opening up the organization to tomorrow's values may appeal to individual employees because they recognize that the new values will accord them a very real sense of professionalism; the union leaders, however, may feel differently. They may believe the proposed changes are false promises designed to cripple the union. Or they may wonder whether the union will even need to exist, because employees will at last be gaining what the union had fought for: real participation in decision making at every level of the organization.

Tomorrow's values certainly change the dynamics of the organization's relationship with the union. Individual employees *have* a voice. They *are* valued. Union leaders who don't justify their own existence through defending members' rights to these values will probably support the pro-

FIGURE 2.1

CORE ORGANIZATIONAL VALUES EMPLOYEE SURVEY

We are interested in your candid views on organizational values. Please indicate how important you think each of the following values should be to our organization.

		Not Important			Very Important	
1.	PARTICIPATION: The opportunity to participate in any decision affecting me.	1	2	3	4	5
2.	DIVERSITY: The opportunity to have my viewpoint taken seriously even when it differs from majority opinion.	1	2	3	4	5
3.	CONFLICT: The opportunity to have my differences in a group dealt with openly and in a safe environment.	1	2	3	4	5
4.	REFLECTION: The opportunity to have the time to question my own thinking as well as that of others in a nurturing environment that suspends premature judgments.	1	2	3	4	5
5.	MISTAKES: The opportunity to make mistakes and view them as just one more way to learn.	1	2	3	4	5

posed changes; however, union leaders who have made their members dependent on the union may be more difficult to work with. They are accustomed to not trusting the organization. Although these union leaders will find it difficult to oppose the values themselves, they will question the organization's sincerity in supporting them. Therefore, conducting an open dialogue with union leaders on the real issues surrounding tomorrow's values is essential. When the union leaders realize that the organization is sincere in its efforts to value employees as contributing, professional members of the organization, they will dismantle the walls they have built and replace them with trust.

Trust will also prevail in the argument over dependency. As employees experience the many benefits of being listened to and valued by the organization, they will realize they don't have to depend on union leaders to protect them from the organization. This is not an argument against the value of unions. Unions offer many advantages to their members. Within the context of tomorrow's values, fighting for rights and dignity just doesn't happen to be one of them.

The School Board. In schools, a third "they" is the school board. Ideally, we should think of the school board and administration as the definition of "we" in the organizational leadership of the school. Realistically, though, this often isn't the practice. So how do I as an organizational leader move the school board from the "they" side of the equation to the "we" side? By dealing indirectly with the issue of power and control. Just like many superintendents, school boards struggle with the issue of power and control. They fear giving up management rights. When they open up the organization along the five value areas proposed here, what assurances do they have that relinquishing power will not be seen as a weakness by their constituents? What safeguards do they have that placing trust in the union will not be eroded by future changes in the union power structure? What legacy of leadership prerogatives does the school board leave its successors? These questions don't have predetermined answers.

The answers lie partially in the faith we place in human beings to treat each other with respect and dignity, along with a system of due process for those who believe their rights are being abused. Since school board members typically have little or no experience operating within the framework of tomorrow's values, leaders must complement faith and due process with solid information about why the organization should be considering the leap to tomorrow's values. Most superintendents or other school leaders have ways to keep the school board current on organizational issues.

Retreats, conference calls, computers linked to school board members' homes, frequent mailings, conferences and workshops, even this book can play a role in educating the board on the merits of considering tomorrow's values. In all likelihood, the superintendent will not be able to guarantee the board any concrete results. But there aren't many guarantees in this business. The best a superintendent can do is provide board members, over time, with the latest research and practice substantiating a strong link between employee participation, employee morale, and employee productivity. Inevitably, letting go of the old and risking the new does become a leap of faith. But by educating the school board members, a superintendent can at least help them see that the risk is a calculated one that will lead to a healthier organization.

CUTTING THROUGH "WON'T LET" AND "ME DO IT"

We've addressed the most formidable challenge in the sentence "They won't let me do it!": understanding and reconciling who "they" are and what they need to move forward. The second piece of the sentence, however, is also important. The words "won't let" imply that others are deciding what I can and cannot do. If I am a leader and "they" are determining what is happening (or is going to happen) without my support to move ahead or without my substantial involvement, then our organization already faces a major problem related to organizational values. We have a power and control struggle going on over who is letting whom do what.

If I cut through the rhetoric and get down to the baseline issue of letting, I realize that "they" aren't in a position to let me or not let me. As leader, I decide for myself the extent to which I choose to exercise leadership in moving us toward tomorrow's values. Simply choosing is not enough, however. There's the very practical question of how to lead in tomorrow's organization, and I will talk about this in detail later in the book.

The third piece of the sentence focuses on me doing it. As mentioned above, I alone am not going to open up the organization. I am going to provide the leadership to create the necessary conditions, but I don't direct happenings in the heart and soul of the organization. We all decide *together* how to implement tomorrow's values.

■ ■ ■

Employees, unions, and school boards can be barriers to change. But they don't have to be. As I've tried to show here, they can be bona fide partners in change.

BRIDGING THE GAP BETWEEN TODAY'S AND TOMORROW'S ORGANIZATION

As we work through how we think and feel about tomorrow's values, we need not feel guilty if we aren't first in line for change. In our leadership roles, we live with the remains of previous unsuccessful attempts at change. Some of the messes we created ourselves. Others were left by our predecessors for us to clean up. In either case, we have justifiable reasons not to jump on the next bandwagon. Consequently, most of us approach with caution the suggestion to abandon today's values.

The gap between where the organization is now and where tomorrow's values could lead us can be measured by the tension we feel in facing the unknown. And certainly most leaders become very tense at the thought of leaving everything up for grabs by giving up their supposed control of the organization. They ask themselves, "How can we be sure the unknown will turn out to be productive for the organization?" The fact is that letting go of the illusion of personal control doesn't automatically cause leaders to let go of their responsibility for the success of the organization. The key to bridging the gap between today's and tomorrow's organization, however, is to remember that in tomorrow's organization, control shifts from personal power to power through living the core values of the organization. Leaders assume responsibility for helping everyone shape those values, which then become the basis for decision making.

In a school, this means that the staff may spend several months developing a core value that focuses on student success. After many hours of reflective discussions, they reach consensus on the following language: "In our organization, we believe all students are important and can be successful, and we won't give up on any of them." The power to shape organizational decisions about teaching and learning pivots on this fundamental value. Whatever these educators do, they first need to be sure their decisions about such important issues as grading, tracking, grade-level retention, and instructional strategies result in practices that are consistent with this agreed-upon value.

The leader assisted in the formulation of the core value by asking questions along these lines:

- What business are we in?
- What do we believe about students as capable learners?
- Why do schools exist?
- What kind of research and best practices should we consider as we develop our value?

Once the core value is in place, the leader also plays an instrumental role in making sure the organization builds in accountability measures to assure that employee performance is keyed to the core value. For example, a group of teachers might regularly review the grade distribution patterns of teachers. And teachers might regularly observe other teachers' classrooms, noting examples of teachers reinforcing successful learning. And supervisory conferences with teachers might focus on the core value of student success.

In summary, leaders don't lose power by opening up the organization. The power resides in the organization being driven by values rather than by events. As a school leader, I must recognize that I don't lose control over the quality of what goes on inside our schools; instead, I have better control of quality because I have strengthened the accountability factor by linking evaluation to core values. Opening up the organization to extensive employee involvement sends a strong message that I, as leader, value employees as professionals. In turn, I hold them accountable for performing in a professional manner.

FIGHTING THE STATUS QUO

Many leaders express concern that we may open up the organization to increased participation and debate, and expend precious energy in this new way of doing business, only to have people say, "Thanks for involving us, but we think the status quo is good enough. It worked well in the past, so it should work just as well in the future." Two safeguards, however, offer some assurance to leaders that people will not opt for the status quo. One is the relentless focus on developing future-oriented core values and holding people accountable for those values. A second safeguard can be found in the process leaders use in creating a *preferred future* for the organization. Chapter 4 elaborates on this process. For now, we can at least have some assurance that opening up the organization does not have to mean putting the organization on the auction block and awarding it to the highest bidder.

Those of you who still have major doubts about the advisability of opening up the organization can be put in two categories: "I don't get it" and "I get it, but I don't need it." Let's look at each of these categories and discuss how you can use important stakeholder information to move forward.

I DON'T GET IT!

"I don't get it!" essentially means I don't see that much difference between today's and tomorrow's organizational values, particularly regarding the implications for successful organizations. At first glance, the differences in the values may seem subtle—too subtle, in fact, to warrant making any drastic change in the organization. After all, virtually everyone can support participation, diversity of opinion, disagreement about issues, time for reflection, and acceptance of mistakes. What is the big difference between the two sets of values?

The difference lies in what we truly believe to be important, not what we give lip service to. The actual values operating within today's organization can be traced to what today's leaders judge to be signs of successful as well as weak organizations. By way of quick review, Figure 2.2 shows signs of strength and weakness based on today's value structure. Tomorrow's value structure flips the measures upside down. As shown in Figure 2.3, the signs of strength in tomorrow's organization resemble the signs of weakness in today's organization. Similarly, today's show of strength becomes tomorrow's weakness.

As you can see from Figures 2.2 and 2.3, there *are* clear-cut differences between today's and tomorrow's organizational values. And, as the figures show, there are significant differences in how we judge successful organizations. Now the question becomes: Which system do I buy into? As you move through the remainder of this book, you should become more able to answer this question with conviction.

I GET IT, BUT I DON'T NEED IT!

The skeptics who say, "I don't need it!" see how organizations would differ under the new value structure, but still believe today's values serve their organization just fine. Many leaders find themselves clustered in this category. They have done a lot of reading on the topic of contemporary leadership. They have heard the high-priced consultants talk about transforming the organization into something fundamentally different. And they respond with a chorus of "Yahbuts" that goes something like this: "Yeah, the reform agenda sounds slick in a perfect world, but we live in an

FIGURE 2.2

SIGNS OF STRENGTH AND WEAKNESS IN TODAY'S ORGANIZATION

Signs of Strength
EVERYTHING'S UNDER CONTROL:

- Employees listen to the organization's leaders and do what the leaders tell them to do.
- Employees' views fall in line with the overall organizational direction.
- Employees communicate a climate of group harmony and happiness.
- Employees convey a climate of decisiveness; firm decisions are made and implemented without looking back.
- Employees concentrate on making no mistakes and working as efficiently as possible.

Signs of Weakness
EVERYTHING'S UP FOR GRABS:

- Employees all over the organization give their two cents' worth on any subject.
- Employees express a variety of perspectives, which are many times in direct opposition to the organizational direction.
- Employees argue about important issues, but resolve their conflicts in a healthy way.
- Employees frequently question organizational leaders and challenge the wisdom of their decisions.
- Employees acknowledge their mistakes and learn from them. Efficiency is not the overriding concern.

FIGURE 2.3

SIGNS OF STRENGTH AND WEAKNESS IN TOMORROW'S ORGANIZATION

Signs of Strength

EVERYTHING'S ON THE TABLE:

- Employees actively participate in any decisions affecting them.
- Employees express a variety of perspectives, even if they differ from organizational direction.
- Employees openly resolve conflict with colleagues in a safe environment.
- Employees question their own and others' thinking in a nurturing environment that suspends premature judgments.
- Employees freely admit mistakes and view them as one more way to learn.

Signs of Weakness

EVERYTHING'S CONTROLLED:

- Employees listen to the organization's leaders and do what the leaders tell them to do.
- Employees' views fall in line with the overall organizational direction.
- Employees always convey a climate of group harmony and happiness.
- Employees understand that once decisions are made, there's no turning back.
- Employees focus on making no mistakes and not admitting those they do make.

imperfect world. As the organizational leader, I am charged with the success of this outfit, in the face of ambiguity and uncertainty about the future. Why should I abandon something that works? The way we work now is successful as measured by the quality of our graduates and by the employees' support for today's value structure." End of chorus.

The challenge issued by this chorus is twofold. First, do the data support our contention that today's graduates measure up to the standards of employers and colleges? Clearly, employers and colleges contend that our students generally don't meet their expectations. The clarion is for a qualitatively different kind of school in the future, operating with a qualitatively different set of values.

The second challenge is to determine employee support for today's values. In fairness to our organization and to ourselves, we need to honestly and openly confront the challenge. It simply is not sufficient to assume that employees support the values leaders believe to be important. We need data verifying that today's stated values reflect what employees really value. Those of you who fall into this category should take the time to ask the people in your organization the questions shown in Figure 2.4. The first two questions relate to the issue of power and control, and the remaining questions relate to the organizational values driving today's organization.

You must consider the administration of this survey to be serious business, for you can't argue that today's values are valued by employees without the data to substantiate that argument. In other words, you need to check out the reality of the organization. Next, you need to use the data as a basis for deciding what the value structure should look like in tomorrow's organization. If employees support today's values and you find that the organizational practices are consistent with these values, then the rest of the book may have little to add to your leadership development. If, on the other hand, the data show questionable support for today's values and a general lack of application of tomorrow's values in the workplace, then the rest of the book should prove helpful.

ONE FINAL NOTE

It's okay to be a skeptic. Trading the known for the unknown can be more than unsettling, it can be frightening. We don't have very many examples of organizations that have let go of today's values, embraced tomorrow's values, and can now show positive concrete results. We do, however, have

FIGURE 2.4
CORE ORGANIZATIONAL VALUES EMPLOYEE SURVEY

We are interested in your candid views on organizational values. Please indicate the extent to which you believe employees in our organization value the following practices.

	Not at all			Very much	
1. Leaders keeping things under control.	1	2	3	4	5
2. Leaders making decisions that will directly affect the day-to-day happenings in the heart and soul of the organization.	1	2	3	4	5
3. Employees listening to the organization's leaders and following through on what the leaders tell them to do.	1	2	3	4	5
4. Employees falling in line with the stated organizational direction.	1	2	3	4	5
5. Everyone in the organization acting as if group harmony and happiness always exist in our organization.	1	2	3	4	5
6. Making firm decisions without ever stopping to reconsider our actions.	1	2	3	4	5
7. Concentrating on making no mistakes.	1	2	3	4	5

many examples of organizations that show positive links between employee participation, employee morale, and employee productivity.

If you still have reservations about jumping out of the box but are willing to look at what's waiting outside, read on. The next chapter will give you more insight into how tomorrow's values will look when they are put in action.

3

PUTTING
TOMORROW'S
VALUES IN ACTION

Imagine that we face a near crisis in our building. Because of continued student growth over the past five years, we are just plain out of room. We have nowhere to house the projected fifty additional students who will be attending our school this fall. And office space is tight because we have added the services of another guidance counselor and part-time secretary. We have already had to convert the school's health office into a substandard size classroom for our English as a Second Language Program, and now we have to decide who else is going to have to give up some of the space they occupy. How do we begin our deliberations? We look to our core organizational values for guidance.

PROCEEDING TO MAKE A DECISION BASED ON CORE VALUES

OPENNESS TO PARTICIPATION

In tomorrow's organization, participation is not just an employee right. We actively promote participation as an expectation for how we do business. We value the process of how we approach issues just as much as, if not more than, the outcome of the decision.

As we approach the issue of overcrowding in our building, we believe it is imperative that all voices be heard in our deliberations. Although we can't legislate participation by everyone, we certainly make it clear that we value participation and want it to happen. We communicate that openness to participation is cherished and valued. It's not just a case of the benevolent leader allowing us to say what's on our mind. The leader does not control the degree of openness. We all work to build openness into the organization. We organize the organization so that participation is integral to the problem-solving process.

For instance, as we tackle the sensitive issue of overcrowding, we begin by making sure the steering committee has at least one member from each stakeholder group: classroom teachers, support teachers, secretaries, and other groups that need representation. During the initial problem-solving process, we create a climate that honors people for saying what they believe, not what they think the organization wants to hear.

Participation can be time-consuming. It can be a nuisance to a leader impatient to reach a decision so the organization can move on to other issues. In tomorrow's organization, however, the overriding values say every person, regardless of classification on the organizational chart, is an equally valued member of the organization; every person is a contributing voice when the organizational philosophy emphasizes that "we are smarter than me." More pointedly, in virtually all cases, we are smarter than the leader.

In the Appleton School District, we encourage members from all employee groups to participate in the various school-based committees focusing on areas such as staff development, budget, and school goals. We even have parents participating in school staff development experiences. We support these practices through an organizational value we have developed about community relations:

> The entire community and the Appleton Area School District should join together in an active and responsive partnership to address educational and community concerns. This partnership should bridge cultural, generational, social, economic, and educational differences and reflect that all community members are valued equally.

OPENNESS TO DIVERSITY

Participation is not enough in tomorrow's organization. We also want the richness of different perspectives. As we work through the problems of overcrowding in our building, we accomplish very little by forming a steering committee made up exclusively of classroom teachers. Granted, we can expect some diversity of opinion even among them, but we need a broader and deeper picture of the issue if we are to make a well-informed decision. People who aren't in the classroom every day have concerns about space, too, and only by including them in our discussions can we get the full picture. If we limit our group to people with common perspectives, we get a narrow picture of the problem and narrow solutions in return.

People doing something as simple as describing the furnishings in a room they're sitting in will describe those furnishings differently simply because each person in the room sees the furnishings from a different place in the room. The combination of perspectives gives us a more comprehensive picture of the reality of what the room looks like. So it is in our school. We don't just ask veteran teachers their views on the space problem. We also ask the custodian, the new teacher of English as a second language, and the secretary. And if we truly value diversity, we have to be willing to let a lone voice carry a lot of weight. For instance, because the custodian has a big picture of all of the spaces in the building, his lone dissident voice may be just as compelling as that of the entire teaching staff in enriching the knowledge base for decision making.

The value of diversity can't be at the mercy of the leader. The power of diversity must be a value conveyed throughout the organization by the evidence that dissident voices make a difference in how decisions get made.

The Appleton School District seeks diverse perspectives in forming committees and project teams. For instance, the president of the teacher's union sits as a fully valued member of the Superintendent's Management Team. Although we have a long way to go, we work hard to encourage our colleagues to speak their mind. That includes telling me, the superintendent, things I don't want to hear. In turn, I pledge to them that I will not shoot the messenger.

OPENNESS TO CONFLICT

Our lives today seem to be filled with conflict. Think about how often the stories you tell your family or friends in the evening touch on conflict at the workplace. Since conflict seems to exist even when we don't want or need it, why would we go so far as to elevate conflict to an organizational value? The question as posed misses the point. Conflict is inevitable; the point is that we can try to keep a lid on it, or we can acknowledge its presence in the organization and build into the organization ways for resolving the conflict in a healthy way. Resolving conflict moves us forward. Keeping it under wraps holds us back.

In the school facing overcrowding, the new teacher of English as a second language and the veteran health room aide become very emotional over which of their services deserves the prime space now occupied by a teaching aide who is a long-time employee of the school and the parent of six children who have attended the school. No one can deny the conflict. The question becomes "How do we resolve this conflict?"

The principal creates a context at the beginning of the problem-solving process by reminding people that territory is a very basic human need. Sometimes we lose our ability to be rational when people start infringing on our space. The principal assures everyone that she will pledge a safe environment for people to speak their piece, even if that means stepping on toes. Staff members know the pledge is a secure one. In the past, the principal has demonstrated fairness and an expectation of confronting conflict openly with no value judgments about who is right or wrong.

So when the sparks fly between these two staff members, the conflict is treated as energy for organizational growth. Demonstrating excellent facilitation skills, the principal asks others to paraphrase what they hear the two staff members saying, then asks how others see the issues being contested. Finally, she asks how the group can resolve the conflict by meeting both sets of expressed needs. At first, they respond, "We can't." The principal replies, "I know, but if we could, how would we do it?" Eventually, the group uses the conflict to create a rich decision linking the two apparently contradictory positions with "and" logic rather than "either/or" logic. In short, they reach consensus (Chapter 5 describes in more detail strategies for reaching consensus).

As leaders, we know we cannot support conflict that leaves the organization dysfunctional. We have all seen the sickness that results from organizations riddled with unresolved conflicts. We aren't talking about that level of conflict here, however. We are simply saying that the gaggle of geese need to honor the honkers who fly out of formation, making lots of noise and calling for a change of path. As long as the honkers are flying north with the rest of the group instead of trying to return south, the conflict can lead to richer solutions.

For example, the Appleton Area School District has in the last several years applied the concept of consensus bargaining rather than the traditional form of adversarial bargaining. Under this approach, we examine issues that significantly affect the way we do business in our district. During bargaining, it is not unusual for members of the union to end up disagreeing openly and strenuously with one another about the issue in question.

The same is true for the school board members. In other words, conflict is recognized as a strength, not a weakness—so long as resolution of the conflict is handled in a constructive way.

OPENNESS TO REFLECTION

Up to this point, problem solving under tomorrow's values appears to be a neat, orderly set of procedures. People actively participate, the group encourages diversity, and everyone accepts the inevitability of possible conflict. The next logical step is to choose from among the most viable positions the one best solution for the organization. Here is where the logic breaks down. Within the space defined by tomorrow's values, we don't simply debate positions until we come up with the right answer. Instead, we expose our own and others' thinking to public examination. In doing so, we need to create a safe environment that insists on suspending assumptions and premature judgments until we have a chance to consider many possibilities, including those not yet contained within the individual perspectives.

Reflection in a safe environment places heavy demands on the organization. By supporting collegial disagreement without personalizing the differences, our organization assures all individuals they can make themselves vulnerable through openly questioning their own thinking. All of us have doubts and uncertainties. Today's organization doesn't encourage this type of self-disclosure. But tomorrow's organization will honor those willing to openly challenge their own thinking. This in turn will lead to a mutual openness where colleagues can challenge one another's thinking as the group seeks a rich solution for the organization.

Because this school truly operates with reflection as an important value, staff members know they can think out loud about their own tentative solutions without being viewed as weak or uncertain. So the ESL teacher says, "You know, I have been questioning the wisdom of teaching the ESL children in a pull-out program. I realize this is the way I was trained and the way I have insisted was best for kids. But I am open to trying a more integrated approach next year within the classrooms throughout the school. This would free up some of this precious space we are arguing about."

It takes a lot of courage for the ESL teacher to tell her colleagues that she is open to challenging the way she has been teaching. By making herself vulnerable, she reinforces the value that it is okay to publicly consider new ways to teach and learn, even if it means questioning our own past practice.

Reflection requires a safe environment. It also requires time. Tomorrow's leaders must realize that the time spent in a reflective environment is a long-term investment, not a short-term expenditure. If we are committed to finding new, more creative ways to address organizational issues in the future, we must also be committed to making the necessary investment in time for reflection.

A few years ago, staff in the Appleton School District expressed the typical frustrations about lack of time to meet and plan. Through the negotiations process, teachers agreed to teach enough additional minutes during the year to allow for early dismissal once a month. Schools now dismiss students before lunch the second Wednesday of every month. Staff use this reflective time for collaborative planning around the theme of student success. In addition, some school teams attend week-long summer institutes to develop and implement their school goals. Schools have even found creative ways to hold retreats during the school year.

OPENNESS TO MISTAKES

Openness to mistakes is an important companion to reflection. It is not enough to reflect on what we think and how we got there. The organization must also be willing to support mistakes as another way of learning. As mentioned earlier, tomorrow's value concerning mistakes starts with the premise that I could be wrong and you could be right. Can you recall very many times in today's organization when you could comfortably admit that you might be wrong—without feeling that you weakened yourself and your position in the eyes of your colleagues? Tomorrow's value publicly supports what we privately know already: We have limitations, we do make mistakes, and we can learn a great deal from our mistakes.

In bringing closure to the discussion about overcrowding, the principal capitalizes on the ESL teacher's idea of integrating the ESL program. The principal asks for teacher reactions to the approach offered by the ESL teacher and, after lengthy discussion, the staff decides to implement this new idea, freeing up a much-needed classroom.

Finally, the principal pauses and says to the group, "What I am about to tell you makes me very uncomfortable. At the last school board meeting, the board supported a request to add an additional classroom teacher at our school because of our projected enrollment growth. These projections were based on data I supplied. Last night, as I reviewed the figures in preparation for room assignments, I discovered that I had failed to take into account the boundary changes implemented by the board. These changes moved seventy children out of our attendance area.

"In summary, I messed up. My miscalculations mean that we will need, at a minimum, one less teacher at our school next year. I could have tried to hide the issue, hoping that enrollment growth over the summer would spare the pain of having to reduce our staff by one position. However, we have created an environment here that says we are better off confronting our mistakes early and openly. And the value applies to me just as much as it does to the rest of the staff. So, I blew it. The bad news is that one teacher likely will not be with us next year. The good news is that we have one less classroom space to create from the overcrowded conditions we face."

Through the ordeal of facing a tough issue, the staff witnessed the principal modeling a core value: It's okay to make a mistake; it's okay to admit that mistake; it's okay to make yourself vulnerable by revealing that you're not perfect and still expect to be valued for your contributions.

Today, openness to mistakes is a rare phenomenon in most organizations. Tomorrow's organization will embrace mistakes as another way of learning. We will take the feedback we get as we discover our mistakes and use it to help us grow, both personally and organizationally.

The Appleton School District has a history of each year giving all staff members their very own "I blew it!" card. Shown below, this card entitles all employees to talk in a safe environment about a mistake they made.

I am reminded of the time a middle-level principal came to see me about his apparent bungling of the new site-based budgeting process. He reached in his pocket, pulled out his card, and said, "I know I'm going to need this today. I've really messed up this budget process." After going through the step-by-step procedures, I said, "Gene, this is exactly the way it is supposed to work out. There are no mistakes here." He quietly reached across the table, took the "I blew it!" card, and slipped it into his pocket. Then he smiled and said, "I have a feeling I may need this little jewel again sometime."

Mistakes Not to Make

The previous section offered a snapshot of tomorrow's values in action. Clearly many different pictures could have been taken, each with different characters, backgrounds, and conditions. In all of them, however, the five values of openness would have remained in constant focus. The pattern of consistently walking the talk where these values are concerned becomes critical in embedding the values in organizational culture.

When we violate our core organizational values—and we will, because we are human—what can we expect? Well, we can expect the organization to react strongly. In fact, we know a value is truly part of the organization when a violation produces anger, disappointment, and hints of mistrust of the violator. As an organizational leader, don't make the mistake of covering up the violation. Acknowledge the cries of mistrust in leadership, the lack of confidence in the values that have been violated, and other such shock waves reverberating through the organization. Don't try to pretend the violation never occurred and don't try to make excuses. Going 75 miles per hour in a 55 mph zone is speeding, regardless of why we were speeding.

If you are the violator, don't make the mistake of sidestepping accountability. Acknowledge the violation and the accompanying responsibility for it, then pledge your continued commitment to the organizational values. People tend to forgive infrequent transgressions. They don't and shouldn't forgive recurring violations. In fact, you need to build into the organization a process of assuring justice, so that frequent violations, including those by leaders, can be questioned in a safe environment.

To see how these guidelines actually work in an organization, let's go back to the school examining the issue of overcrowding. Put yourself in the principal's shoes. You call together the steering committee addressing the issue of overcrowding. Without your knowledge, the teachers have met privately the previous day and drafted a position statement calling for all nonclassroom staff to receive secondary priority when assigning room space for next year. At the steering committee meeting, the teacher group presents the position statement and calls for a vote. Since teachers comprise a majority of the seats on the steering committee, the motion passes. So much for equal participation by all who have a stake in the issue.

Now what do you do? Those of you looking for ways to prove tomorrow's values won't work might use this violation as proof that teachers can't be trusted to always behave in ways consistent with the values they have agreed to. Therefore, you might feel justified in reverting to the old ways of doing business. This would be a mistake. Is this how you would want the teachers to respond if you were the violator?

The best way to approach this problem would be for you to treat the violation as a "systems issue" (systems problems are discussed in detail in Chapter 6). In other words, the teachers' action signals that more work needs to be done to find out what people believe about power and control. More work needs to be done to create a safe environment for constructively dealing with conflict and to discourage the use of back-room power politics.

In summary, don't make the mistake of tossing out everything you as a group have worked for because someone has violated the values. As difficult as it may be not to take the setback personally, seize the occasion to help the entire group reflect on what happened and how they can grow from the apparent step backward. Three steps forward and one step backward still leave you a step ahead.

Another mistake to avoid is allowing tomorrow's values to justify extreme forms of behavior. For example:

- Openness to participation by all does not justify repeated dominant behavior by any individual.
- Openness to diverse perspectives does not justify a pattern of anti-organizational, disloyal behavior from anyone.
- Openness to conflict does not justify rude, unprofessional conduct.
- Openness to reflection does not justify repeated, extreme attempts by an individual to stall decisions by saying we should take more time to think about the issues.
- Openness to mistakes does not justify an extended pattern of sloppy performance by any employee.

One last caveat: As an organizational leader, don't place yourself in the untenable position of being the only person responsible for deciding when someone's behavior is out of line. As mentioned previously, make sure you build into the organization a process whereby the group assumes accountability for calling into question unacceptable behavior.

LEARNING FROM TOMORROW'S LEADERS TODAY

Although few in number, leaders who support tomorrow's values and have made significant progress in pulling them all together do exist. If we are wise, we will look to them for guidance, for they have much to teach us. Doing so may make us feel inadequate and defensive, but learning from others' successes is an important part of tomorrow's values. It is a part of the culture of openness, and we need to find ways to make it happen on more than just a surface level. We need to learn from more than just the final, polished product. We need to learn from the pain and pitfalls encountered on the road to success. We need also to find out how successful organizations cleared many of the hurdles we expect to encounter on our journey. In short, we need to skip the show-and-tell part and get on with the how-it-happened part. By looking to those who have paved the way, we genuinely honor them. And all of us benefit from the resulting exchange of ideas and support.

4

CREATING A

PREFERRED FUTURE

Imagine approaching your favorite hardware store early on a Saturday morning just as the owner, Mr. Arnold, is placing the OPEN sign on the front door. Mr. Arnold begins another day selling the products and services that have earned him a long-standing reputation for quality. That reputation didn't come easily, though. Twenty-five years of daily placing the OPEN sign on the front door. Twenty-five years of consistent, even persistent, pursuit of Mr. Arnold's vision for being the community's most dependable and comprehensive hardware store.

Imagine now an alternative scenario. Ten years ago, you approached Mr. Arnold's store on a Saturday morning just as he was rearranging shelves to make room for a bakery section. Five years ago, Mr. Arnold added a dry cleaning pick-up station in the rear of the store. And today, as you make your way up the sidewalk to his store, you notice the TOTAL HARDWARE sign has been replaced with a neon sign blinking ARNOLD'S PHARMACY, BAKERY, DRY CLEANING, AND HARDWARE. Yes, Mr. Arnold is placing the OPEN sign in the front window as usual. But open for what? When questioned on this subject, Mr. Arnold says he had not planned to add to his original design; things just unfolded as friends and neighbors pressured him to cater to their individual wants.

As we consider opening up our organization along the five aspects of openness discussed in this book, putting the OPEN sign on the front door of our organization isn't enough. We have to know and clearly convey what business we are in. We can't continually rearrange our shelves and add specialty lines to our main business. We need to look to the future and decide how we plan to get there.

PUSHED BY THE PAST OR PULLED BY THE FUTURE?

In the face of the uncertainty and ambiguity permeating much of our lives, one thing is for sure: the future is out there. It's waiting for us. We have first-hand experience proving that the future eventually becomes the present and then the past. We cannot skip the future, but we can decide how we will shape it.

Unfortunately, many of us choose to have the future shaped for us. By not consciously acting on the forces that give meaning to our future, we become the consumers of what others feed us. We opt into a passive role, letting someone else determine what the future holds for us. Just as in Mr. Arnold's case, this option may be the path of least resistance, but it certainly isn't the path that tomorrow's leaders will choose.

Even if we choose to actively shape our future, we still have some choices to make. Do we arrive at the future being pushed by the past? For most organizations, the answer is yes. Centuries of being pushed into the future seem to have worked well. The belief that today and tomorrow are logical extensions of yesterday gives leaders a sense of security. Because they know what yesterday was like and are generally happy with it, today's leaders choose the low-risk option of planning tomorrow on the basis of what has already worked well for them.

Tomorrow's leaders will see things differently. Tomorrow will not be simply an extension of the past and the present. The exponential explosion of knowledge, technology, and other factors contributing to the rapids of change destroy any remaining hope and security that tomorrow will be a faster paced version of today. Tomorrow will not be pushed by the past; tomorrow will be pulled by the future.

This does not mean that we should ignore the past. We should continually be alert for ways to honor those who were instrumental in shaping today's reality. The norms, values, and history of our organization can be found in stories, heroes, and rituals that have deep, personal meaning to veteran staff members. The richness of the past should be part of the mosaic of the future. But the exact pattern of the past need not be that of the future.

Seizing on this fundamental shift in worldview, tomorrow's leaders will approach the future in a radically different way. Rather than rely on outdated strategic planning models that forecast the future based on the past, they will relentlessly create *a preferred future* by imagining what could be and letting the pull of the imagined future lead the organization through uncharted waters to get there.

What are the implications for leadership of creating a preferred future? Well, the very idea of *creating* calls for an entirely different approach to leadership. "Creative" is not a word most leaders today would use to describe their leadership style. Yet abundant creativity resides in each of us. We don't use it because today's organization discourages the kind of environment that frees the creative potential to dream, imagine, and mentally play with ideas. We always have the barriers of the past and present haunting us.

Think how much more refreshing it would be to create tomorrow rather than extend yesterday. All of us have the creativity to mold a preferred future, a future we ourselves determine. Why should we endure someone else's future? Tomorrow's leaders must make sure that planning for the future builds in the preferences and dreams of the members of the organization. People must be free to shape their destiny.

Putting it all together, tomorrow's leaders will provide the context for people to create a compelling future. This future then becomes the pull that leads us out of the present and leaves behind the anchors of the past. The power of a preferred future invites even the most reticent to become excited. The next step is figuring out how to get there.

BEGINNING WITH CORE VALUES

Whether we are in the hardware business or the school business, we can't create a preferred future without knowing what we stand for. So many organizations try to be all things to all people and end up being nothing to anyone. They become driven by events, flitting from one innovation to another in search of the magic box that, once installed, will never have to be unplugged again. In schools, the magic box can take the form of mastery learning, management by objectives, total quality management, outcome-based education, transformational leadership, and on and on. When the magic box doesn't immediately produce the intended results, leaders tend to pull the plug, scrap the box, buy a new and different box, and hope for the best. Eventually, people expect the magic box to fail, and thus put no effort into helping it work.

Tomorrow's organizations will reject the event-driven philosophy and substitute a value-driven approach to creating a preferred future. The core organizational values become the pull to the future, leading the organization toward a vision of excitement and energy. Much has been written about the "V-word," vision. Leaders are encouraged to design visions, share visions with their staff, and develop mutual understandings of what the vision will look like in practice. But talking about creating a future and developing a vision is squishy stuff. It's difficult to get a handle on where to start, how to proceed, and what the final product will look like.

Unfortunately, vision making is often mistakenly translated into writing a two-paragraph mission statement during a half-day workshop and then waiting for this statement to propel the organization into the future. Without downplaying the importance of the development of a mission statement, creating a preferred future is much more complex and comprehensive than writing a mission statement. We can see exactly how by examining one organization's path to creating a preferred future.

CREATING CORE VALUES IN APPLETON, WISCONSIN

Beginning in 1988, the Appleton Area School District administration launched a multiyear commitment to become value-driven. With over 12,000 students and 1,200 employees, it was difficult to know where to start. After much discussion, I recommended that the core organizational values should be initially developed by those directly accountable for modeling these values in the organization. Therefore, the fifty-seven administrators began a four-year process of creating core values. The monthly all-administrator meetings were transformed into leadership development sessions, and arrangements were made with a nearby university to award graduate credit for this leadership development work.

Applying the most current research and best practices from sources such as Covey (1990), Senge (1990), and various publications from the Association for Supervision and Curriculum Development, administrators talked extensively about what they valued. A combination of individual reflection, small-group work, and large-group discussion set the context for reaching consensus over a four-year period on a set of core organizational values. In the remainder of this chapter, we will look briefly at the series of steps the district took to become a value-driven organization.

STEP 1: UNDERSTANDING CORE VALUES

Constructing core values can be like trying to catch smoke in a net. The proposed values often seem to quickly become porous and without substance, so that we run the risk of gaining nothing for all our efforts. To reduce the risk, the Appleton Area School District participated in some activities designed to help us better understand the meaning of core values.

First, we asked ourselves, "What is the definition of core values?" For our purposes, we defined core values as statements reflecting our firm convictions about why we exist. Core values are not observations, perceptions, or operating rules. They are things we believe to be extremely important to our organization. They are characterized by descriptors such as:

- Fundamental,
- Guiding,
- Philosophical,
- Pointing the way.

Core values help answer such questions as:

- Who are we?
- What do we stand for?
- What business are we really in?
- What is most important to us?
- Where do we want to go in our preferred future?

Sample core values include statements like:

- Quality instruction and other related services should be our primary focus for achieving student success.
- The power to make decisions and effect change should be distributed throughout the organization via access to support, information, and resources.
- Risk taking and innovation should be supported as a way of achieving organizational improvement.
- Diversity should be valued and evident in our school district.

Simply reading words isn't sufficient to understand the nature of core values. Developing a deeper understanding of the concept comes from interacting with colleagues to determine what meets the test of a value. The Appleton Area School District administrators used the exercise outlined in Figure 4.1 to help provoke discussion leading to a clearer picture of what constitutes a value. Returning to the criteria stated earlier, only items 3, 4, and 7 in this figure meet the test of true core values. The other statements are important ideas, but they represent a mixture of observations, forecasts, and practical suggestions.

FIGURE 4.1
CORE VALUE EXERCISE

Check the statements below that meet the criteria for core values. You don't necessarily have to agree with the value in order for it to meet the criteria.

_____ 1. High school students should be in scheduled activities every period of every day.

_____ 2. School districts should experience increases in elementary enrollment in the next several years.

_____ 3. Equity should be a primary basis for providing learning opportunities to all students.

_____ 4. School districts should allocate resources with students foremost in mind.

_____ 5. School districts should offer staff development opportunities during the school day.

_____ 6. Schools should experience increased diversity and complexity of student needs during the next decade.

_____ 7. Students should be active participants in their own learning.

Many organizations develop mission statements, vision documents, and other lofty-sounding paragraphs about the future direction of the organization. This work is an important first step in constructing core values. All too often, though, it is the only step the organization takes.

Staff members in the Appleton District found that an additional step is critical. Although they agreed that a statement like "Our district is passionately committed to student success" is a clear enunciation of values, they wanted more. They wanted to know what implications such a statement would have for practice in the district. So the administrators added another step to the process of developing core values. For each core value, they developed *guidelines for decision making*.

Guidelines for decision making are decision rules that give practical meaning to the core value. In other words, the guidelines say what the organization *will do* based on the organizational commitment to the core value. Examples of guidelines for decision making related to the core value concerning student success include the following:

- We will develop critical thinking, creative thinking, and problem solving.
- We will emphasize exploration and discovery as integral to each student's school experience.
- We will convey to each student, "You are important, you can succeed, and we will not give up on you."
- We will expect all students to develop a strong work ethic.

Without the step of developing guidelines, core values typically come across as abstract, academic statements absent any direction for how the organization should function. With guidelines added, the core value takes on a much richer meaning. Appendix B offers some guidance for identifying core values.

STEP 2: DECIDING WHERE TO START

In the Appleton Area School District, deciding which values to initially address wasn't easy. The mission of the school district, achieving student success, seemed a likely candidate in developing an initial value; however, the administrators concluded that the proverbial question of power and control should be resolved first. Their reasoning was that unless we reach consensus on our values regarding empowerment and decision making, we run the risk of filtering all the other values through the old hierarchical model of control.

District administrators spent about ten hours over a three-month period working and reworking the language that best reflected what they believed about empowerment. The result was consensus on the following statement:

> The power to make decisions and effect change should be distributed throughout the organizational structure of the district by providing the necessary support, information, and resources. Participatory decision making should be integral to the effective functioning of our school district.

Consistent with the points made above, the administrators realized that the value statement standing alone could become hollow rhetoric. So they took the second step of developing guidelines for decision making, a series of "will" statements saying what employees will do to make the Empowerment value come alive in their organization:

- We will involve employees who have expertise and/or interest in decisions that are relevant to them (e.g., staffing, budgeting, curriculum, materials selection, and staff development.)
- We will involve students, parents, and the community in the decision-making process.
- We will design organizational structures that encourage multiple points of view and interaction beyond the typical departmental or school boundaries.
- We will train employees for leadership roles in the decision-making process.
- We will encourage decisions to be made as close to the point of implementation as possible, with consideration being given to those accountable for that decision.

These words may seem to you like any other words in print. For the Appleton staff, however, the core value and accompanying guidelines take on special meaning. The words say what the district believes about empowerment. With this value firmly in place, the district now has a future pull, a vision for how meaningful interaction and decisions will occur in various settings in the district. As new ideas such as site-based management appear on the scene, we don't react in event-driven fashion to try to decide whether to install another magic box. Instead, we use our core value of Empowerment as a reference point for decision making. We organize our communication and decision-making structures to align with this value. And we ask, "Does this innovation reflect our core value?"

STEP 3: DEVELOPING ADDITIONAL VALUES

After lengthy debate, argument, and listening carefully to colleagues with varying points of view, the Appleton administrators reached consensus on what they believe about empowerment. They didn't stop there, however. The administrators methodically applied the approach outlined earlier to develop core values and guidelines for decision making in seven areas:

- Empowerment and decision making
- Risk taking
- Diversity
- Reward and recognition
- Quality
- Community building
- Student success

Four years passed before the set of core values was completed. But use of the term "completed" is misleading. Although the seven values and guidelines for decision making were now in print (see Appendix A), there remained much work ahead to help embed the values in the culture of the organization.

STEP 4: MAKING MEANING FROM WORDS

After decades of being part of aborted efforts to change people and organizations, the Appleton administrators realized that each individual, department, and organization needs to create personal meaning from an abstract idea before meaningful change occurs. Applying this fundamental principle of change, the Appleton administrators spent time individually, in small groups, and in the large group talking about the meaning of the words they crafted. To illustrate the process used, we will trace the steps applied to developing the core value concerning recognition and reward.

Realizing that fifty-seven administrators can't productively write a core value, we assigned administrators to subgroups of about seven members. Each group was composed of representatives from various departments and grade levels and remained an intact work team during the school year. One of the subgroups volunteered to work on the core value of Recognition and Reward and eventually submitted the following language to the entire administrative group during one of the leadership development sessions:

The Appleton Area School District shall recognize individuals for their accomplishments and/or contributions in support of the common goals of the District.

Within their subgroups, administrators discussed the meaning of the core value and offered language changes to better capture what the entire group believed. One small group presented this suggestion:

We believe that the accomplishments of individual employees are vital to the health of the organization and the successful attainment of its goals and mission.

Lengthy and lively debate ensued. Emerging from this dialogue, which spilled over to the next meeting a month later, administrators agreed on common language that had personal meaning to them:

The accomplishments of individual employees should be valued and recognized in order to promote the health of the organization and the successful attainment of its goals and mission.

The administrators agreed to let this "final" draft linger for about two months before examining it one more time. Upon reexamination, some administrators felt strongly that the value should say something more specific than "successful attainment of its goals and mission." The group reached consensus on wording changes and the following statement became the core value to be passionately defended by the group:

The accomplishments of employees should be valued and recognized in order to improve the quality of instruction and related services to our district.

The process outlined here is time-consuming. Those who want quick action get impatient. If we intend to be driven by values rather than events, however, investing time and energy in the short run will pay dividends in the long run. Value-driven organizations don't collect the useless magic boxes that clutter event-driven organizations.

STEP 5: DEVELOPING SHARED COMMITMENT TO THE CORE VALUES

Developing core values is essential to creating a preferred future, but the process does not end there. Another critical step is leading the transition from a personal vision to a shared organizational vision. There is no one route to success. In Appleton, district administrators concluded that it would be a token gesture to try to involve all 1,200 employees in the initial construction of core values. They decided instead to involve those most directly assigned the leadership for the district. Once the values were developed and approved by the school board, the administration used various forums for discussing the values, including sessions attended by all employees, annual reports, and school faculty meetings. The point of these forums was not to convince employees to believe in the values, but to clearly and consistently articulate the preferred future envisioned by district leaders.

Using the core values as a guide, schools began to take selected core values and rewrite them to make them more personally meaningful. For instance, Appleton West High School spent considerable time involving students, parents, and staff in discussions about student success. Incorporating the district value and comments from various perspectives, the staff developed their own value concerning student success:

> As a staff we are committed to the success of each student. We are committed to working with students, parents, and each other to create a school in which EACH STUDENT:
>
> • is welcomed and valued as part of a caring, educationally challenging environment;
> • feels good about himself/herself and personal accomplishments;
> • desires to be actively involved in the academic and co-curricular programs of the school.

The staff developed an additional seven statements indicating what student success means to Appleton West High School. They also created a series of statements about the expectations for staff members within an environment emphasizing student success. You and I may have generated a completely different set of words to convey our meaning of the concept of student success; however, as long as we were consistent with the district direction and our work was based on current research and best practices, our statements would be applauded. The Appleton West High School staff concluded their work with a powerful summary statement:

> If we create a school where students, staff, parents, and community work as one, this vision will become reality and Appleton West High School will be a school where each student and staff member will be successful.

Other schools used the core values in developing school goals related to a vision for the future. Some of the central office departments used the core value model to develop statements reflecting their own vision of a preferred future. As the momentum continued for articulating what the district and its various groups of employees stood for, one element anchored all the efforts: the district's core values. In other words, schools and departments began to develop their own value statements within the district's framework of values. People were free to compose any value statements that did not conflict with the basic direction of the district's values. For example, an elementary school staff could develop a core value about how empowerment will involve parents, students, and staff. And this value may look different from the neighboring school's value on the same topic. No school, however, could develop a core value that said the principal knows best, because this would not be in keeping with the district's value concerning empowerment.

STEP 6: ALIGNING PRACTICES WITH VALUES

It's not enough to embed values into the culture and stop there. We must constantly ask ourselves, "To what extent do our practices match our core values?" As long as we use our core values to gauge our course to the future, we have a steady referent to help shape our practices. In addition, the guidelines for decision making deliberately focus on what we will do relative to each value. The "will" statements outline expectations for preferred practices.

After developing the first three core values, the Appleton administrators decided they had better do a reality check with the schools. So they asked schools to use the format outlined in Figure 4.2 to find out how important these values and guidelines were to school staff and to determine the extent to which the values were implemented at the school site. The data collected were used exclusively by the school to identify areas of inconsistency between stated values and actual practices.

As one illustration of this process, Wilson Junior High School noted some discrepancies between values and practices, and in response they developed the following school goal: "The goal of the Wilson school community will be to promote interaction between staff members that will encourage individuals and groups to initiate risk taking, innovation, and experimentation without fear of failure." The faculty then identified a set of activities to achieve their goal.

FIGURE 4.2
ASSESSMENT OF VALUES AND PRACTICES

Listed below are a core value and guidelines for decision making related to our school. Indicate how important you believe each of the items in this chart should be to our school. Also indicate how effectively each item is being implemented in our school.

IMPORTANCE

IMPLEMENTATION

Not Important				Very Important		Not Effective				Very Effective
					Core Value					
1	2	3	4	5	Risk taking and innovation should be supported as a way of achieving organizational improvement.	1	2	3	4	5
					Guidelines for Decision Making					
1	2	3	4	5	1. We will encourage individuals and groups throughout the organization to initiate risk taking, innovation, and experimentation.	1	2	3	4	5
1	2	3	4	5	2. We will create an atmosphere where people can make and acknowledge mistakes without fear of "failure."	1	2	3	4	5
1	2	3	4	5	3. We will recognize individuals and groups for taking risks to further the mission of the district.	1	2	3	4	5

FIGURE 4.2—*Continued*
ASSESSMENT OF VALUES AND PRACTICES

IMPORTANCE		IMPLEMENTATION

Not Important — Very Important		Not Effective — Very Effective
1 2 3 4 5	4. We will recognize that short-term setbacks may in turn result in long-term personal or organizational growth.	1 2 3 4 5
1 2 3 4 5	5. We will expect and support evaluation of experimental and innovative practices and encourage wider implementation of successful programs.	1 2 3 4 5
1 2 3 4 5	6. We will encourage the sharing of results from experimental or innovative practices and programs, whether they are successful or not.	1 2 3 4 5
1 2 3 4 5	7. We will consider conflict a sign of a healthy organization and will resolve conflict in a spirit of fairness, respect, and trust.	1 2 3 4 5
1 2 3 4 5	8. We will encourage individuals with appropriate expertise to consider new assignments, even though these assignments may differ from past career paths.	1 2 3 4 5

This continuous assessment of congruence between values and practices is one of the highest quality forms of accountability. As we create a preferred future for our school or department, we also create a set of expectations for ourselves that we truly own. We have no one else to blame or depend on for meeting the requirements. We are accountable.

We also have to listen to disquieting words when we don't walk our talk. This became particularly evident to me when I proposed an administrative reorganization plan and did not involve the staff in the development of the plan. Despite my reasoning for why involvement was inappropriate, there was a huge outcry that the core value of shared decision making had been violated. In other words, the value had been embedded in the culture of the organization and employees rightfully expected everyone, including me, to live up to the value.

STEP 7: MAKING CONNECTIONS FOR NEW STAFF

Moving to a value-driven organization takes time, and in the process, staff members inevitably come and go. Something must be done to help assure that the values of the organization don't exit with those people leaving the organization. True organizational stability hinges on the extent to which the values shaping our preferred future transcend the personalities of the people providing leadership at any point in time.

In the Appleton Area School District, a series of sessions was designed to focus on the core values of the district. District staff used the seven core values as a base for developing a program to introduce all new employees to the heart and soul of what the district stands for. These sessions are a powerful tool for assuring that the preferred future stays prominent in the minds and actions of everyone, even the new employees.

STEP 8: CREATING YOUR OWN FUTURE

Throughout this chapter, the experiences of the Appleton Area School District were used to illustrate the process of creating a preferred future. But the Appleton model is not the only way. It may not even be the best way, particularly for your organization. The fundamental principle is that each organization must have a clearly conveyed process for creating a vision for the organization. It can begin with dreams of what your unit will look like five years from now. It can begin with constructing one core value, then another, and another. It can be born out of reflection or out of crisis.

The point is that it must begin. We can't shape a preferred future by waiting until we have all the answers. That time will never come. By acknowledging that we will make mistakes along the way and that we will sometimes spin our wheels, we are free to take the critical step of inventing a future we can call our own.

5

DECIDING HOW

TO DECIDE

In organizations governed by today's values, deciding how to decide isn't very complicated. Generally, decisions are made by the boss. Even in instances where employees' ideas are accepted, the supervisor ultimately decides for the group. When power and control remain central values in the organizational culture, decision-making power lies at the top of the organizational chart, and decisions trickle down the chart.

In tomorrow's organization, decision making gets turned upside down. The old ways of doing business are challenged in the face of new values calling for group decision making. But the values themselves don't tell the whole story. Group decision making can suffer from its own entanglements. We'll try to sort out some of them by addressing basic questions related to organizational decision making.

HOW DO DECISIONS GET MADE?

There are several ways decisions can be made. One way is for the supervisor to decide. Although this option is not often used in tomorrow's organization, it does have a place in the repertoire of decision making; we'll discuss the specific place later in this chapter. Another way is to not actively decide at all. Failure to take action on an issue is, by default, a decision. This option, too, is rarely used in an environment that encourages participation. Voting is a familiar and democratic approach to decision making. It is efficient for groups, generally nonconfrontational, and simple to understand. All it takes is a call for the vote and a count of the "ayes" and "nays." The outcome is known almost immediately, and majority wins.

The idea of consensus is a relative newcomer to the options for decision making. Consensus means the group reaches a collective decision that virtually everyone can support. Although the slogan of consensus decision making offers inherent appeal, the process possesses its own set of problems. Later we will explore these problems and how to overcome them.

WHO DECIDES HOW TO DECIDE?

In deciding how to resolve this issue, we turn once again to our core values concerning openness. Do we truly believe that the power to make decisions and effect change should be distributed throughout the organization? Do we believe that the collective expertise of the staff makes for wiser decisions than the expertise of the person at the top of the management chart? Do we believe that empowerment is most effective when people have access to the support, information, and resources to get the job done? In other words, do we believe in opening up the organization to participation? At this point, the answer should be yes. Therefore, it logically follows that *the group should decide how decisions get made throughout their part of the organization.*

WHAT ISSUES DESERVE GROUP ATTENTION?

Granted, not every single issue deserves group attention. In arriving at an answer to the above question, organizations need to be sure they don't slide back into the power and control trap. It is tempting and natural for individuals (including the supervisor) to see discussion of this question as an opportunity to return to the old values. As supervisor, if I control which decisions are eligible for group discussion, I essentially have returned power to myself. A similar regression occurs when a management council manipulates the system so that all group recommendations must be approved by the council before a decision is declared official.

Assuming we believe that the organization should involve all employees who have an interest in discussing issues that affect their professional lives, almost any issue becomes fair game for group discussion and decision making. During the growing pains of adjusting to tomorrow's values, we can anticipate that some groups will want to declare all categories of decisions open for group resolution. For instance, one school staff insisted that everyone sit together to debate every issue facing the school, including the flavors of soft drinks in the vending machine and the color of the cover of the parent handbook. As trust grew within the group and time became even more precious, however, the staff decided that some decisions could be handled by the principal, and others could be assigned to the school management council. In other words, group decision making does not automatically translate into whole-group decisions on every issue arising in the course of a week. Routine items and emergencies, for instance, don't lend themselves to calling a group together for a decision.

Likewise, issues that are determined to be important for group consideration do not always require the presence of every group member. Mandating participation runs counter to the spirit of opening up the organization, so people may choose not to participate in the discussion of an issue; they may even elect not to attend scheduled meetings. Inserting this provision into the ground rules for group decision making honors each person's judgment in choosing among competing priorities and allotting time and energy.

Along with the individual's choice to decline participation on a particular issue comes a promise from the supervisor and the rest of the group not to play "gotcha" with the individual. In other words, people should not sit in judgment of a person's choice, nor should they hold that choice against the person in future discussions. At the same time, the right to choose carries with it a major responsibility. Specifically, if I choose to opt out of our group's decision-making process, I by default opt into endorsement of the decision and its implications for my work life. Otherwise, "gotcha" gets played in reverse: I can try to use my absence from the discussion as power to block the group's progress until I get caught up on all the facts.

To illustrate the point, suppose I choose not be involved in deliberations about next year's school goals. After numerous meetings and small-group work, the proposed goals are submitted to the entire staff for consensus to move ahead. I object strenuously to the omission of a school goal about improved playground behavior. Due to my absence during the goal-setting meetings, I fail to realize the staff had already considered and rejected the idea of playground behavior as a goal. The principal reminds me that I opted out of the process, so I must opt into the staff recommendation.

As long as the group clearly defines the ground rules for participation and balances the individual's right to opt out with the group's right to move ahead with a decision, surprises and power plays will be kept to a minimum.

How Does the Group Decide?

This discussion focuses on decisions that are appropriate for the group to make. Two basic options exist: the group can vote or they can reach consensus. As mentioned earlier, voting offers several virtues. It also presents a major drawback: When the majority wins, the minority loses. And the minority can be as much as 49 percent in opposition to the decision. Voting promotes a win-lose mentality that leads people to use whatever strategies are necessary to secure votes, thus taking us back to the power and control model for organizational decision making. If we are serious about opening up the organization, we need to realize that voting takes us in the opposite direction because it too often closes the organization to authentic participation, diversity, conflict, reflection, and mistakes.

The Meaning of Consensus

In the previous sections, several basic questions about organizational decision making were posed and answered. There remain, however, some lingering questions about the meaning of consensus. Ideally, the spirit of consensus means that we reach a collective decision, one that everyone supports after openly and extensively considering the many diverse facets of the topic being discussed. It does not mean that we find the lowest common denominator of the group's ideas, agreeing to the little piece of common ground found among the many, varied perspectives of individuals. Consensus means seeking higher ground, creating a new solution that incorporates and at the same time goes beyond individual perspectives. Consensus decisions clearly illustrate that all of us are smarter than any one of us.

The Road to Consensus

In tomorrow's organization, we need to realize that groups won't reach quality decisions via shortcuts. The road to consensus can best be negotiated by adhering to the values concerning participation, diversity, conflict, reflection, and mistakes.

OPENNESS TO PARTICIPATION

The strength of consensus decisions rests in part with encouraging everyone in the group to become serious contributors to the problem-solving process. But participation is more than just talking. Consensus building requires that we honor the right of each colleague to be heard without interruption, in an environment of trust and open communication. This calls for a commitment by each individual to be genuinely interested in what is being said.

OPENNESS TO DIVERSITY

The consensus process requires that everyone listen to all points of view, acknowledging that even the most unpopular viewpoints deserve fair examination. In the old value structure of organizations, diversity was seen as a deterrent to good decisions: If you and I disagree, I need to convince you to come around to my way of thinking. In tomorrow's organization, the value of diversity is turned upside down: If you and I disagree, I need to listen intently to your perspective. I can learn why you think the way you do about a certain issue, and the perspective I gain will help us make a better group decision. When we all think alike, our discussions follow a narrow path, devoid of the diverse views that enrich truly collective decisions.

OPENNESS TO CONFLICT

As discussed in Chapter 1, today's values emphasize the appearance of harmony, whereas tomorrow's values incorporate conflict as an inevitable and potentially healthy part of life. As facilitators move groups toward consensus, they watch intently for signs of conflict. When they find it, they move toward the tension and not away from it. Conflict brings out the deepest differences in perspectives. It amplifies the diversity among group members and contains the seeds for a solution unimagined by any one person.

Conflict won't be visible if the organizational culture reflects the belief that the appearance of harmony is central to an effective organization. How many times have we pretended that everything was wonderful at work, though in our gut we ached because of some unexposed conflict? To achieve strong group decisions, we have to move beyond false harmony and openly acknowledge conflict. Beyond just acknowledgment, however, we need to deal with conflict in a constructive way. We need to move to the tension point and make conflict work for us, not against us. If we separate the issues from the personalities, and if we have the necessary training to handle group conflict in a constructive way, we can use conflict as positive energy in pursuit of our goal: a strong collective decision. Obviously, this level of risk taking requires a safe organizational environment. Later in this chapter, we'll look at one model for creating such an environment.

OPENNESS TO REFLECTION

Without question, consensus building takes time. In fact, the time factor alone causes some groups to revert to the old decision-making models of voting or letting the boss decide. Then they wonder what went wrong, as their organizational culture again becomes dominated by power and control thinking rather than empowerment thinking.

Tomorrow's organization will constantly struggle to find reflective time for groups to deliberate important decisions. One key to embracing consensus is to avoid bringing petty or subgroup issues to the large group for discussion and decision. As trust within the group grows, people will do a better job of identifying those issues needing collective reflective time.

Valuing reflective time in reaching consensus means valuing the time to talk things out until virtually all serious objections to a unified course of action have been resolved. Consensus requires suspending judgments and premature positioning. As discussed many times in this book, when we take positions and defend them zealously, we reduce the likelihood of reaching a group decision incorporating the best of individual perspectives. In tomorrow's organization, creating reflective time for consensus building helps assure that we achieve two fundamental goals of lasting decisions: a shared knowledge base and group ownership for the decisions made.

OPENNESS TO MISTAKES

Consensus building occurs in an atmosphere that encourages people to think out loud about the universe of possibilities available for reaching a decision. As we stray from the most logical solutions to those that have never been dreamed, we make ourselves vulnerable to sounding foolish. Tomorrow's organizational values celebrate "far-out" thinking and the possibility of not having the right answer.

Similarly, consensus includes the possibility that the group decision could be wrong—or that it at least might not be the best possible solution. This belief becomes critical as we wrestle with the question of what to do about those individuals who steadfastly oppose the direction in which the vast majority of the group is heading. As I discuss more fully in the next section, a group decision shouldn't be held hostage by one or two strongly dissenting voices. At the same time, openness to mistakes means that the vast majority of the group could be wrong. In order to move ahead and concurrently honor the minority view, we must assure that the entire group will revisit the issue in the future. Setting a specific time for review is helpful—six months, two years, or whatever seems reasonable to the group, especially those who hold the minority perspective. Such assurance gives those who don't support the original consensus decision the opportunity to be heard again.

UNTANGLING COMPROMISE, CONSENSUS, AND UNANIMOUS CONSENT

Even groups who consistently apply the principles of consensus decision making sometimes drift from consensus to compromise. When we compromise, we give up something we stand for in order to receive something in return. Operating under compromise conditions, problem solving may unfold something like this: "The Board will compromise its belief in standardized work hours if teachers will agree to supervise recess daily."

Unlike compromise, consensus requires the flexibility to step away from defending positions and, instead, move forward on what the group as a whole wants to accomplish and how the group wants to get there—together. Working within a framework of consensus, problem solving takes a different slant: "How can the Board and teachers honor the status of teachers as professionals and, at the same time, expect teachers to perform certain nonteaching duties to best serve our students' needs?"

On a more personal level, compromise forces me to trade in something I value in order to get something else I value a little more. Reciprocally, you do the same thing. We both compromise on what we value. In consensus building, however, we search for a solution based on the following thesis: There is a solution yet to be discovered that allows each of us to maintain the integrity of our values while finding agreement.

Consensus sometimes gets confused with unanimous agreement. Admittedly, the spirit of consensus suggests that we find a solution we can all happily support. In reality, we can expect occasions when repeated attempts to reach a workable solution end up with some individuals steadfastly opposing the "consensus" point of view. For instance, consider the issue of ability grouping at the middle school level. Let's suppose that after three months of deliberations, a review of the research, and discussions with other schools, 10 percent of our school staff still insist on ability grouping for every subject. With all due respect to the 10 percent who favor ability grouping, it is unfair to hold hostage the momentum for moving forward just because the proposed solution does not reflect unanimous agreement.

In anticipation of these circumstances, groups need to establish a ground rule within their consensus-building principles that addresses a last-resort measure. For instance, the group could agree that a group decision will be declared if at least 85 percent of the staff support the solution. The establishment of such a ground rule needs to be accompanied by two assurances. First, the 85 percent ground rule will never be applied until we have asked ourselves the following questions concerning tomorrow's organizational values:

- Have we *fully* involved everyone as participants in the problem-solving process?
- Have we listened *carefully* to all points of view, particularly the unpopular perspectives?
- Have we *seriously* faced any emerging conflict in our group and conscientiously tried to reconcile our differences?
- Have we *thoroughly* exhausted all possibilities for a quality decision, allowing ample time for reflection?
- Have we *openly* acknowledged that I could be wrong and you could be right, clearing the way for a solution that is stronger than any one perspective?

Out of respect for the professional judgment of the minority perspective, a second assurance needs to be granted: The group decision will be revisited within a specified time period, and the dissenting voices will again be listened to carefully. This provision minimizes the idea of winners and losers by assuring a second hearing. It also signals the flexibility of the group.

In adopting a last-resort ground rule defining consensus as a certain percentage of yes votes, group members owe it to themselves to make sure the ground rule is clearly *a last resort*. In other words, it should never become a shortcut for getting a quick vote and moving on to other matters.

ARE CONSENSUS DECISIONS BINDING?

The answer to this question lies in understanding the distinction between shared governance and shared decision making. Shared governance assumes that all members of the group have an equal vote in governing the organization, resulting in equal accountability for actions. While this sharing of power has implicit appeal, groups need to come to grips in a practical sense with the level of accountability they want to assume. For instance, does the school staff (as a group) want to be held accountable for dismissing a colleague for sexual misconduct? Does the central office department want to be held accountable for changing the schedule of the night custodian? Does the school management council want to be held accountable when an irate parent complains to the school board that her theater group was denied access to the school auditorium? If not, these decisions then fall under the umbrella of shared decision making. In shared decision making, everybody contributes to the process of decision making, but only one person is held accountable for the decision.

Applying this line of thinking to a specific school, it is the principal who will finally answer for the decisions made at the building level. In rare instances, therefore, a principal who simply can't defend the group's decision as being in the best interests of the students or the district may exercise "veto power" over a consensus decision. To better understand the implications of this apparent power, we need to know what is considered *rare instances*. Although we run the risk of setting arbitrary standards here, it seems reasonable to expect that at least 95 percent of group decisions should happen *with* consensus and *without* veto. If a pattern of veto occurs, the principal and the principal's supervisor need to start examining whether such practices are consistent with the values of the organization.

Instances of power grabbing within a school's consensus framework aren't limited to the principal level. Some teacher unions want to denounce site-based decision making as a camouflage for site-based recommending. They claim that true site-based decision making occurs only when the school staff as a group make the final decision. Those who believe in tomorrow's values for opening up the organization would entertain such a possibility, so long as accompanying performance accountability is directly connected to the responsibility for making the decision.

TRAINING FOR CONSENSUS BUILDING

One of the worst forms of empowerment occurs when we turn people loose to implement tomorrow's organizational values without the necessary training to be effective in the new environment. Even if we truly believes in the values associated with opening up the organization, we can't automatically change our behavior. Cast into a group setting that calls for consensus decision making, we find ourselves with nothing but the old rules to rely on. The old rules invoke old behavior, so we resort to power and control tactics because that's all we know how to use in situations of group conflict. Disaster results. We make ourselves vulnerable by trusting the new values, and then we get hurt because win-lose strategies emerge when the old value system kicks in. Consensus gives way to power plays and factions jockeying for their positions to prevail. People walk away mistrustful, blaming each other as well as the consensus process. In the future, they decide, they will return to the old way of doing business because in that arena they at least know how the game is played.

To avoid such disaster, don't omit the training necessary to make consensus work. Many different consensus training models are available to help groups work together effectively. There is no single recipe for success. There are, however, some basic training guidelines to look for in any program. The model discussed below illustrates how these guidelines have been successfully applied by several school districts.[1] This model requires very few resources: a trained facilitator, enough chairs for everyone (no tables), easels with flip charts to accommodate groups of five to seven people, and an appealing meeting environment.

GUIDELINE 1

Honor the right of each colleague to speak without interruption in an environment of trust and open communication.

Most of us have learned the hard way that groups frequently lack an environment of trust and open communication. In a consensus-building model, these important ingredients are developed as the facilitator moves the group through a series of steps. For example, the facilitator might begin with a grounding activity that asks all group members to do the following:

---

[1]Major credit for this model belongs to friend, colleague, and teacher, Bob Chadwick.

- Introduce themselves.
- Describe their connection to the group.
- Comment on how they feel about being at the meeting.
- Describe their expectations for the meeting.

This simple grounding task is a powerful tool for setting the expectation that each person will be heard without interruption. How often do we begin a meeting with everyone being able to comment in an environment that is respectful of each statement, regardless of the speaker's status in the organization? The grounding also establishes verbal territory for each participant, allowing his or her voice to be entered into the discussion pool early in the process. This initial commentary makes it easier for people to speak later in the process.

Grounding also acknowledges that people bring feelings to the group. These feelings could be baggage from previous experience with the group; they could be strong emotions about the topic to be discussed; or they could be emotions related to something that happened at home just prior to the meeting. Whatever their basis, feelings play a significant role in problem solving in an environment of trust and open communication. The grounding acknowledges the importance of feelings without pressing people to reveal intimate, personal thoughts that are best left unsaid.

As a follow-up to the grounding activity, facilitators typically use both small-group and large-group activities to move people forward to the resolution of the issues at hand. With each activity, group members develop greater assurance that they can speak and that their remarks will be listened to with respect. The role of the facilitator is crucial in establishing this safe environment, particularly with groups just embarking on the consensus-building process.

GUIDELINE 2

Move to the point of tension and begin problem solving in a nonthreatening way.

Generally, our tendency is to avoid tension in group settings. We want to mask the possible conflict and talk about more superficial issues. The facilitator should listen intently for the real issues of the group, and ask several people representing various perspectives to talk about what they think and how they feel about the issues. Both rationality and emotion are important in arriving at collective decisions. The facilitator should also help people become able to separate the issues from the personalities involved, freeing them to see tension as a positive energy that can lead us out of gridlock toward a solution we can all support. As people begin to realize that they can speak safely on a given issue, they tend to make themselves more vulnerable. Showing our vulnerability allows us to be seen as individuals rather than anonymous positions on the organizational chart.

GUIDELINE 3

Focus on best-case outcomes and press for creative solutions to achieve these outcomes.

Too often, our problem solving centers on the barriers to success by trying to prevent the worst-case outcomes from happening. The more barriers we tear down, however, the more barriers we seem to discover. This approach to problem solving generates negative energy by pressing harder and harder against the restraining forces. A training model for consensus decision making does not duck the worst-case outcomes. In fact, the model includes a step at the beginning of the problem-solving process that asks the question "What are the worst-case outcomes of not solving the problem?" By dealing with worst cases at the beginning, people are better able to answer the follow-up questions: What are the best-case outcomes of solving this problem? What are creative solutions for making the best-case outcomes happen?

For virtually every group, the best solutions to the group's problems already exist within the expertise of the group. The facilitator is trained to connect various individual perspectives with "and" thinking so that the collective wisdom is harnessed to reach a rich collective decision.

GUIDELINE 4

Use a variety of problem-solving tools to move the group toward consensus.

Some groups come together and talk about a problem until they get too tired to do anything but make a hurried decision so they can go home. Though they have good intentions, they don't have a good stock of useful tools. The consensus model uses an array of problem-solving tools to help reach consensus. Depending on the size of the group and the nature of the issue, the facilitator can lead the group through activities such as nominal group process, fist-to-five consensus seeking, silent group sorting of ideas, collective statements, determining priorities by spending tokens, and mapping cause and effect using branching diagrams. Appendix C provides a brief description of these activities. In the Appleton Area School District, we have conducted sessions on how to use these problem-solving tools for staff members representing virtually all employee groups. Appendix C also provides a brief description of these activities.

■ ■ ■

The above guidelines barely scratch the surface in describing the power of training for consensus building, but they are a beginning any school or district can build on. In the Appleton Area School District, we have received a grant to train every employee in this model of consensus building and conflict resolution. In addition, we have trained a cadre of about twenty-five facilitators who are available to work with schools or teams that request outside help to resolve internal disputes. Each year, we offer a two-day training session for all new administrators and other employees who volunteer to participate. We even provide, on a limited basis, facilitators to other districts who are struggling with issues requiring trained assistance.

As stated earlier in this chapter, there are no shortcuts to reaching quality group decisions. Consensus building takes time, perseverance, and above all, commitment to the values related to opening up the organization. Is it worth all the effort? Groups who have implemented the concepts outlined in this chapter swear they will never go back to the old way of making decisions. Some have even trained their own internal facilitators, who are available to work with groups in the organization on consensus training and conflict resolution. The goal? To embed the value of consensus in the organizational culture.

6

LEADING THROUGH

SYSTEMS THINKING

W hen things go wrong in today's organization, leaders go hunting for people to blame. They have been indoctrinated in the belief that people are the causes of problems and that problems are solved by swiftly correcting the behavior of the "problem" employees. If problems persist, leaders generally believe that their only recourse is to fire the "problem" employees.

In tomorrow's organization, problems will be viewed much differently. Throughout this book, the emphasis has been on opening the organization to participation, diversity, conflict, reflection, and mistakes. When it comes to problems, tomorrow's leaders will open the organization in another way: They will open the organizational *system* itself to examination as a possible cause of problems. In short, leaders will shift away from blaming problems on individuals and move toward ferreting out the problems that are inherent to the system at work in the organization.

Although the concept of systems thinking has been around for decades, the language and tools of systems thinking have been by and large obscured in complex and intricate formulas and diagrams. In this chapter, we will look at a framework that will enable tomorrow's leaders to take the basic principles of systems thinking and apply them to real-life organizational problems. We will review guidelines for better understanding systems thinking and then apply the guidelines to a case study involving a school district's struggle with a systems problem.

UNDERSTANDING SYSTEMS

The first step in understanding systems is to work from a common definition of the term: A system is a collection of parts that interact to function purposefully as a whole. The best way to draw meaning from this string of words is to contrast examples of what is and is not a system. For instance, a collection of parts in the back room of an auto repair shop is not a system. Nor is a structure assembled from those random parts; it may be a piece of art or a piece of junk, but it is not a system. By assembling particular parts so they work together to produce power for operating a lawn mower, however, we create a system.

A system must include parts that interact in a purposeful manner, and this interaction must produce a whole that is greater than the sum of its parts. The lawn mower engine is more than the individual parts lying in the back room; it is a functional system that becomes a nonfunctioning heap of parts if any significant piece is missing.

Applying this definition of a system to organizations, we find that anytime we bring together people and materials to achieve an organizational purpose, we create a system. Most systems exist within larger systems. A teacher, a classroom, some instructional materials, and twenty-five children constitute a system. Fifteen of these systems within a building form a larger system called a school. And eighteen of these schools make up a school system. The school system, in turn, is part of a larger, more complex system serving the needs of the families living in the community. We can even work our way into systems as complex as a universe. For now, though, we will focus on the concept of systems designed to educate our children.

GUIDELINES FOR APPLYING SYSTEMS THINKING

If we really want to resolve problems in our organization, we must move systems thinking from academic discourse to meaningful practice. The following guidelines will help you apply systems thinking in your own organization:

- Focus on the system, not the people.
- Learn how the current system evolved and how it connects to related systems.
- Expect the system to resist interventions meant to disrupt the stability of the current system.

• Evaluate the system against the organization's core values.

• Look beyond symptomatic problems and symptomatic solutions to fundamental systems issues.

• Think whole-system, long-term solutions and allow time for the solutions to take effect.

• Anticipate new systems problems arising from current systems solutions.

In the remainder of this section, we'll look at how each of these guidelines can be successfully applied toward organizational improvement.

Guideline 1: Focus on the System, not the People.

Most workers are well-intentioned people who are simply trying to perform as best they can what they understand their duties in the organization to be. Teachers, for instance, usually are trying to conform to ideas about teaching and learning that were taught to them in education courses and that were developed and reinforced in their work with students in schools. As criticisms mount regarding the quality of education provided in our nation's schools, the typical response in today's organization is to search for people who aren't pulling their weight—even though they may be doing exactly what they were taught to do—and then "fix" them or fire them.

In tomorrow's organization, the response to perceived problems will shift. For instance, if we think the quality of schooling is not meeting changing expectations about what constitutes student success, we need to identify our new expectations, then redesign our systems to provide teachers the training and support to meet the new expectations. Instead of blaming individuals for doing what they were hired to do, we need to make long-term adjustments by focusing on system changes.

Let's look at another problem scenario. Imagine that a school district is losing talented administrator candidates to surrounding school districts. The superintendent blames the staff of the human resources department for not pursuing candidates aggressively enough and warns them that if they continue to let qualified people slip through their fingers, heads are going to roll.

Tomorrow's leaders will see this problem quite differently. They will move the organization away from blaming the staff of the human resources department and move toward an examination of the entire system involved in recruiting, interviewing, and selecting administrators. By changing the system to become more aggressive in advertising positions, by shortening the time line from posting positions to hiring, and by offering more competitive salaries, the issue will be addressed systemically and the people involved in the hiring process will not become the scapegoat for the organization's problem.

GUIDELINE 2: LEARN HOW THE CURRENT SYSTEM EVOLVED AND HOW IT CONNECTS TO RELATED SYSTEMS.

Some leaders rush to tackle pressing problems without considering how the system in which the problem exists was put together in the first place. For instance, imagine a school board member being elected on a platform of saving taxpayers money. The board member volunteers to serve on the teacher negotiations committee in hopes of presenting compelling, rational evidence for why the teachers should settle for a modest salary increase. To the board member's surprise and disappointment, final decisions regarding teacher salaries have little to do with an individual board member's powers of persuasion and everything to do with how comparable districts have settled their negotiations. In addition, if the teachers union and the school board reach an impasse, a third-party mediation system goes into effect to settle the dispute.

This board member could have more effectively channeled her energy by learning the history of teacher negotiations in the district and the role of the mediation system. With such background information, she would have been well-situated to negotiate from a position of strength rather than naïveté.

In tomorrow's organization, leaders will find that time spent learning the history of the system and its connection to related systems is an investment in quality systems solutions for the future.

GUIDELINE 3: EXPECT THE SYSTEM TO RESIST INTERVENTIONS MEANT TO DISRUPT THE STABILITY OF THE CURRENT SYSTEM.

Stability is one of the hallmarks of a working system. Every system incorporates defense mechanisms that protect it from the constant bombardment of stimuli trying to disrupt its stability. In most cases, the harder the pressure against the system, the harder the system pushes back to resist change. When today's leaders meet resistance to change, they think, "Okay, if you want to play hardball, I'll show you how hardball is really played!" Instead of trying to understand why they are meeting resistance, they prepare themselves to aggressively do battle with the system to see who will prevail. With this mindset, it's usually the entrenched ways of the system that win.

For example, suppose a new high school principal is hired with a mandate from the school board to put in place interdisciplinary team teaching. The principal brings in highly touted speakers on the subject of integrated learning. He regularly attends high school departmental meetings to try to convince teachers of the merits of this new way of teaching. He also eliminates the position of the high school department chair, replacing it with grade-level chairpersons. Within six months, the principal reports to his supervisor that the staff has organized against him and is doing everything possible to sabotage his efforts to bring about change. In short, the system is resisting outside threats to its stability.

Suppose, however, the principal introduced the idea of interdisciplinary team teaching by acknowledging that the teachers were opposed to it and then inviting teachers to tell him exactly why they were opposed to it. He appeals to the teachers union and school board for waivers to the teachers' contract, which discourages teachers from taking such risks as accepting new, experimental class assignments. The principal also provides the incentive of additional release time for groups of people willing to initiate interdisciplinary team teaching. In other words, the principal works *within* the system to remove barriers and increase incentives. Although the process of making individual adjustments to the system is slow and arduous, it is generally more successful than fighting against the entire system all at once.

GUIDELINE 4: EVALUATE THE SYSTEM ACCORDING TO THE ORGANIZATION'S CORE VALUES.

Too many of today's organizations are driven by events. Leaders hop from one quick fix to another, skipping the important step of determining what business the organization is in and what it stands for. Consequently, when problems occur, the leaders have no enduring values to guide their problem-solving efforts. Because they have not identified the common purpose toward which all the organizational systems should be working, they try to solve problems by arbitrarily tinkering with the parts. When their blind tinkering causes even bigger problems, they inevitably resort to blaming the people who have been following their lead all along.

Let's look at a concrete example of an event-driven organization. Suppose Anderson Elementary School is having trouble with parent acceptance of the elementary report card. A vocal group of parents wants the school to give letter grades so parents will have a more realistic view of their children's performance. In fact, some parents want actual percentages, such as

94 percent, assigned to each subject area on the report card. Accordingly, the school changes the report card.

Three years later, parents want effort grades assigned to each subject. The school again changes the report card. Two years after that, the district redraws school attendance boundaries due to major population shifts. The parent population of Anderson School changes markedly, and this new group of parents wants to return to a more narrative report card. What will the school do now?

Let's shift gears and imagine that Anderson Elementary School is now using systems thinking in making decisions. The staff recognizes that there is disagreement about how report cards should describe student progress. They also realize, however, that report cards are only part of a system centered on the idea of student success. Consequently, they decide to examine their fundamental beliefs about student success, including discussions about how to measure it and how to communicate standards for success to students and parents. They involve parents in this examination of beliefs and reach consensus on a core organizational value concerning student success. Then they describe how the system—including report cards—should work to reinforce this core value.

The development of a core value concerning student success puts this staff in a much better position to examine system problems that may arise in the future. Any fundamental changes can now be considered in the light of this core value. Necessary changes should be well received, since the staff members (and the parents) have already agreed on the value and examined the system accordingly.

GUIDELINE 5: LOOK BEYOND THE SYMPTOMATIC PROBLEMS AND SYMPTOMATIC SOLUTIONS TO FUNDAMENTAL SYSTEMS ISSUES.

Too often we latch onto an apparent problem within a system and attempt a quick fix. In complex systems, especially, the competition for scarce time, energy, and other resources pushes us to quickly identify a problem, solve it, and move on. For example, suppose teachers start complaining that the district is being left behind while other school districts are moving to site-based management. The teachers union begins sending memos to the superintendent and the school board inquiring when the district is going to involve teachers in decision making. Even parents get into the act and ask about their involvement in future decisions. Letters appear on the editorial page of the local newspaper, and teachers union officials speak up at school board meetings.

Feeling the pressure, school board members ask the superintendent what the district is doing about site-based management. Taking the hint, the superintendent sends ten staff members to a workshop sponsored by the state department of education. In addition, a team from another school district speaks to the superintendent's advisory council about the merits of forming school improvement teams and developing school governance councils.

Addressing the issue of site-based management, the superintendent directs all schools to develop school improvement teams within three years. Also, he says that the governance of each school will be handled through a school council comprising teachers, parents, and the principal. Each person gets one vote on school issues brought to the council. With these mechanisms in place, the superintendent is satisfied that the system issues have been addressed and resolved. When relationships among teachers, parents, and administrators deteriorate further, the superintendent starts blaming people for not following through on the directed organizational changes.

Where did things go wrong here? For starters, the superintendent paid attention to the symptomatic problem: not having site-based governance in place. If the superintendent had followed Guideline 4 (concerning core values), he would have discovered that the fundamental issue was teachers' and parents' desire to be viewed as people with worthwhile contributions to make to the decision-making process. The superintendent made another mistake by proposing a symptomatic solution. He recast organizational structures without first confronting the issue: What are this district's fundamental beliefs about the participation of stakeholders in the decision-making process?

In tomorrow's organization, the superintendent will work toward a solution that reflected these fundamental beliefs, creating forums for constituents from various perspectives to discuss how their needs for participation can best be met within the organization's core values. After the needs have been identified, the superintendent will provide direction in making sure that the organizational practices are consistent with the core values.

GUIDELINE 6: THINK WHOLE-SYSTEM, LONG-TERM SOLUTIONS AND REMAIN PATIENT FOR THE SOLUTION TO TAKE EFFECT.

As discussed previously, a system can be found in a space as small as a classroom or as large as a universe. The temptation in today's organization is to focus on the system most apparently in need of attention. To illustrate, let's examine some apparent scheduling problems associated with adopting the middle school model of schooling.

The junior high scheduling model is fairly straightforward. Every teacher teaches six periods a day, five days a week. Teachers who do not have enough sections to warrant a full-time contract may pick up an additional section at the high school level. Under the middle school arrangement, scheduling is more complicated. Teachers are expected to team-teach in blocks of time up to four hours in length. This model does not neatly accommodate teachers in need of an additional section to complete a full-time contract. It also requires rethinking how certain subjects, such as music and foreign languages, can fit into block scheduling instead of the traditional period scheduling.

With all of these possible headaches, the approach today's leaders usually take is to give up on the new system and stick with what works. Tomorrow's leaders will adopt a different strategy. First they will ask, "What are we trying to accomplish philosophically with the middle school model?" Once the organization has clarified these values, it will look at all the systems affected. Scheduling is only one consideration. Other systems include integrating subject areas, incorporating the student advisor concept, and providing common team planning time. As leaders help the organization identify solutions, they will need to keep in mind that the middle school concept can't be implemented overnight. They are looking at a minimum commitment of three years of the district's resources to implement the new system.

Finally, such a commitment will require patience to see the solution through to completion. In the short run, the fundamental solution won't be very gratifying because it creates immediate headaches without assurance of long-term success. If leaders can stay focused on the whole-system, long-term solution, they can resist the temptation to slide back into dwelling on short-term problems like scheduling that only produce symptomatic solutions. Instead, leaders will focus on what they're trying to accomplish for students, and approach the barriers within this context.

GUIDELINE 7: ANTICIPATE NEW SYSTEMS PROBLEMS ARISING FROM CURRENT SYSTEMS SOLUTIONS.

We often spend so much time and energy getting our fundamental solutions in place that we have little tolerance for any problems incurred from implementing the solution. We have gone to great lengths to convince others that a given solution is the most effective one for our particular system. We have offered assurances that the overall system will benefit from significant long-term results. Then we get blindsided by new problems.

More specifically, our advocacy blinds us to the inherent drawbacks of our solution.

Returning to the middle school dilemma discussed above, imagine that we finally get school board and school staff support to move ahead with this new system. Two years later, as we put the final touches on the staffing patterns, we realize that this new model will cost the district $300,000 in additional staff. Suddenly, we are faced with a new systems problem.

This is the way systems work. Look at the automobile. Although it eliminated some of the problems of earlier modes of transportation, it created a new problem, air pollution. Likewise, possible solutions to the problem of the federal deficit create new problems related to taxing and spending policies for this country. And providing ample opportunities for school staff to participate in important decisions generates other problems, such as finding the time to make this happen. Our challenge is to *anticipate* the issues arising from implementing new systems solutions, alert others to the downside of implementing the new solutions, and prepare to accommodate the new problems.

■ ■ ■

In this section, I have outlined seven basic guidelines for applying systems thinking to organizational problems. Although brief guidelines cannot include every aspect of implementing systems thinking, they do provide a framework for moving from theory to practice. By using systems thinking to tackle the challenges of the future, an organization can learn to develop more effective, proactive, and long-term solutions to problems. In the next section, I describe how such an organization might work.

THE ROSENDALE SCHOOL DISTRICT APPLIES SYSTEMS THINKING TO SPECIAL EDUCATION ISSUES

The Rosendale School District is a fictitious yet typical school district facing changing conditions in its special education programs.[1] Current enrollment in the various programs continues to climb at a rate that has

---

[1]Major credit for developing this case study belongs to friend and colleague William Joy.

school officials worried. Over the past ten years, the number of students in the programs has doubled, and in response, the district has added staff, classrooms, materials, and plenty of headaches.

This week, the superintendent received a report showing that referral rates this year have increased 15 percent over last year. Superintendent Bellows believes it's time for action. She calls together a group of seven key staff members and explains the conditions. She recommends that the group begin initial problem solving using the guidelines presented in this chapter.

GUIDELINE: FOCUS ON THE SYSTEM, NOT THE PEOPLE.

As the superintendent's ad hoc group starts discussing the special education issue, the conversation quickly turns to puzzling over the pattern of referrals. Which schools are heavy referral schools? Which teachers seem to most readily submit referrals? Who is complaining about the way we are doing business now?

Superintendent Bellows reminds the group that they have lapsed into the old way of doing business. She refocuses the discussion on the system, not the people. She suggests that they begin by developing a common understanding of related history.

GUIDELINE: LEARN HOW THE CURRENT SYSTEM EVOLVED AND HOW IT CONNECTS TO RELATED SYSTEMS.

The Director of Special Services provides a brief history lesson. Over the past twenty years, state and local education agencies have received financial incentives for students qualifying for special education services. The incentives, however, fall far short of the actual costs for special education absorbed by the district. In other words, the special education budget has increased much faster than the overall district budget.

Besides special education legislation and corresponding litigation, another primary but subtle system is influencing special education enrollments: the general education system. With increasing numbers of students at risk for achieving success in school, the general education system has more frequently turned to special education for help. This dependency has produced almost parallel systems within the district.

The Director reminds the group that the district's current system of special education centers on special education teachers providing special instruction to special groups of students in their own special classrooms for most of the school day.

GUIDELINE: EXPECT THE SYSTEM TO RESIST INTERVENTIONS MEANT TO DISRUPT THE STABILITY OF THE CURRENT SYSTEM.

In the Rosendale School District, the system of referrals for special education can be described linearly as follows. A classroom teacher expresses serious concerns about a child's performance and ability to succeed in the regular classroom. The student is referred for placement into a special education program. The student meets stated criteria and is placed in a special education class. The classroom teacher is satisfied that the student's needs will be more appropriately met with special help. The special education teacher is satisfied that he has an opportunity to provide special help. Parents are pleased that the district has been so responsive to the student's needs. The word spreads about how satisfied everyone is with the placement and, not surprisingly, the referral rates escalate across the district. Figure 6.1 outlines the influence relationship occurring. With this cycle of apparent satisfaction and success, why would anyone in their right mind attempt to disrupt the stability of the current system?

FIGURE 6.1
SPECIAL EDUCATION SYSTEMS CYCLE

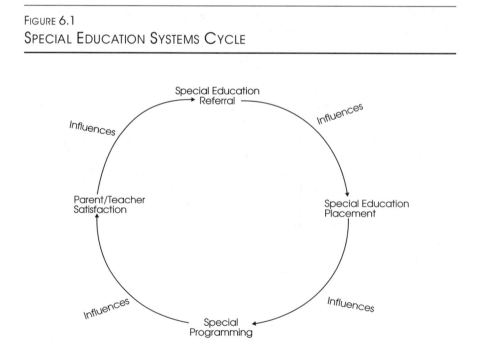

GUIDELINE: EVALUATE THE SYSTEM ACCORDING TO THE ORGANIZATION'S CORE VALUES.

Superintendent Bellows asks the group to consider seriously the question above: Why would anyone want to disrupt the stability of the current system? One of the principals refers to a document on the wall expressing a core value of the district: "You are important, you can succeed, and we will not give up on you." The superintendent recalls that the school board recently approved another core value developed by the district staff that endorses an integrated learning environment as beneficial for *all* students. The Director of Special Services says the district has also pledged that all students will be treated with dignity, respect, and worth.

This discussion spills over into three more meetings focusing on these questions: What do we hold as core values regarding student success for *all* students? Are our practices consistent with our beliefs?

GUIDELINE: LOOK BEYOND THE SYMPTOMATIC PROBLEMS AND SYMPTOMATIC SOLUTIONS TO FUNDAMENTAL SYSTEMS ISSUES.

During the continuing discussion on the topic of special education, someone raises the following question: Is the increase in the number of students receiving special education the problem or a symptom of the problem? The group noted that the intent of the legislation was to ensure that all students with disabilities would be afforded a free, appropriate public education in the least restrictive environment possible. They also thought that the advocates as well as the writers of the legislation could not have anticipated that such a large number of mildly handicapped, under-achieving students would be referred and found eligible for special education services.

Not long after the special education legislation was passed, the group noted, student demographics began to change. Classroom teachers faced more diversity and increasingly complex student needs. There was a greater mismatch between teacher expectations and student performance in classrooms in the Rosendale School District. In fact, said the group, this mismatch is really the fundamental problem. Special education, with its accompanying incentives, simply provided a quick fix. The problem-solving group concluded that the quick-fix solution is now pervasive in Rosendale and, by its very nature, has prevented the district from pursuing a more fundamental solution, one that would have a greater, longer lasting effect on the problem.

The group also concluded that the district's core values hold the key for arriving at fundamental solutions. And they pointed out that fundamental solutions have a built-in delay factor; the positive effects of fundamental solutions take much longer to appear than the positive effects of symptomatic solutions. The superintendent cautioned everyone not to be swayed by the temporary relief supplied by quick fixes.

GUIDELINE: THINK WHOLE-SYSTEM, LONG-TERM SOLUTIONS AND REMAIN PATIENT FOR THE SOLUTION TO TAKE EFFECT.

Just as it was necessary to use a systems approach in analyzing the special education issue, it was equally imperative to use a systems approach in applying leverage that would allow the Rosendale School district to implement whole-system, long-term solutions. As an outgrowth of the meetings called by Superintendent Bellows, several district committees accepted the challenge of examining current district practices and recommending a broad set of strategies to address the fundamental problem. Although their work is far from complete, here are some of their preliminary thoughts:

• More broadly educate our entire staff on the board-approved core values and their implications for practice.

• Indicate how the district's commitment to reorganizing by school clusters will have a positive effect on the provision of educational services for *all* children in the school cluster.

• Discuss the implications of site-based management in making decisions about the distribution of resources to best serve students.

• Assure that school-based planning teams represent the perspectives of students with disabilities.

• Outline the necessary staff development needs for *all* staff as fundamental solutions are proposed.

• Remove systems barriers and excuses that block the district's movement to fundamental solutions.

• Remain patient and committed to the core values. Don't take the easy way out!

Committees will continue to add meaning to the above suggestions and then present concrete plans of action so the district can move forward.

GUIDELINE: ANTICIPATE NEW SYSTEMS PROBLEMS ARISING FROM CURRENT SYSTEMS SOLUTIONS.

As organizations methodically engage in systems thinking, they simply cannot afford to dismiss this last guideline. All the progress made can be eroded and even eliminated if the organization fails to anticipate new systems problems. The Rosendale superintendent knows that there will be a significant downside to implementing new solutions. Some of the new difficulties include:

• Rethinking the roles of administrators, special education teachers, and support staff.

• Breaking the dependency relationship between general education and special education.

• Creating additional time for joint problem solving around the needs of individual children.

• Addressing the barriers posed by state bureaucracies and legislation.

• Allaying the fears of parents and teachers who found satisfaction with the old solutions and now fear that gains on behalf of students with disabilities will be lost.

• Using mistakes along the way as excuses to return to the old way of doing business.

• Proving that student performance will be any better under the new system.

Despite these potential problems, the Rosendale staff remains convinced that the core values concerning student success will be better served by the proposed fundamental solutions than by quick fixes. Indeed, with these guidelines and suggested strategies in place, the Rosendale School District is well on its way to using systems thinking to solve fundamental systems issues. By applying the ideas presented in this chapter, your organization could be too.

7

LEADING WITHIN THE PARADOX

E ven under the best of circumstances, leading in tomorrow's organization won't come easily. It will be a constant struggle resulting in large
part from the changing conception of leadership. Each of the previous
chapters captures a piece of the struggle and includes ideas for overcoming
it. But there is one more piece that we haven't yet looked at. It is the
difficulty of wrestling with paradox.

PARADOXES AND HOT FUDGE SUNDAES

A paradox is a thought that seems to embrace two opposing ideas at
the same time. It tempts us into either/or thinking, asking us to choose
between two ideas. Will it be stability or instability, control or freedom,
group or individual effort? As we will discuss later, how we confront and
answer these apparent contradictions dramatically affects our success as
leaders.

Our first encounters with paradoxes occurs in childhood. We cut our
teeth on either/or thinking. Parents and society teach us to think in absolute
terms: good or bad, right or wrong, safe or dangerous. Choosing between
opposite or competing values becomes our template for decision making.
Reward and recognition follow those who learn to make the "right" choice.
Being right boosts our test scores and our chances for advancement.

Author's Note: This chapter is adapted from Jerry L. Patterson, "If Not Now, When? If Not
Us, Who?" in *Reflections: 1992.* Cambridge, Mass.: International Network of Principal's Centers, Harvard University, 1992.

As adults, we sharpen our skills on the same stone. Either/or logic dominates our approach to making decisions. Faced with winning or losing, cooperating or competing, having or not having, we feel we must decide between the two apparently contradictory choices. We must exclude one option from further consideration.

Back in the old days of so-called abundance, we could get away with exclusive thinking. If we chose "this," we could return to the well and pick up some of "that" later if we needed it. Tomorrow things will be different. In times of resource scarcity, choosing "this" now will preclude us from picking up some of "that" later. This scarcity mentality generates survival thinking and behavior. Either/or choices mean something is lost, usually forever. Such thinking tends to polarize people and paralyze thinking. We're all fighting for the biggest slice of the pie. As individuals, we walk away either a winner or a loser. As an organization, we all lose.

In tomorrow's organization, however, we don't always have to make competing choices. Returning to our childhood for a moment, suppose we are told we have a choice between a hot dessert and a cold dessert. Suppose, as well, we prefer hot and cold at the same time. Ordinarily, such a preference would be greeted with, "Make up your mind, child. Do you want a hot dessert or a cold dessert?" But what if we see other possibilities? What if we let go of either/or thinking and grab onto the energy of "and" thinking? We might find riches. We might find excitement. We might find something as wonderful as . . . a hot fudge sundae—a truly delicious idea that's the result of a combination of seemingly incompatible elements.

How Do We Measure Success?

Tomorrow's leaders excel at creating hot fudge sundaes. They call upon their capacity to hold apparent contradictions (A or B) simultaneously in their mind, linking them with "and" thinking instead of either/or thinking. "And" logic moves us from *exclusive* thinking to *inclusive* thinking.

Of course, this kind of thinking is easier said than done. But, again, nobody said leading in tomorrow's organization would be easy. Inclusive thinking does not come naturally. As we confront paradoxes along the way, we tend to think about them as we were taught to when we were young. That is, we try to resolve the tension of the paradox by eliminating one part of it. In doing so, we clear up the ambiguity—but only temporarily. By denying one half of the paradox as real, we get symptomatic relief. We simplify by choosing option A over option B. As discussed in Chapter 6, however, tomorrow's leaders will not settle for symptomatic solutions.

In the long run, the denied piece of reality (option B) lurks in the shadows, waiting to be found again. Once discovered, option B becomes more difficult than ever to reconcile in the light of alleged progress on option A. Applying this approach to problem solving, leaders will face increased tension as they stare once again at apparently competing choices, with even higher stakes riding on this either/or proposition.

To turn paradoxes from millstones to milestones in the leadership journey, tomorrow's leaders must see them as kindling for their fire. When a paradox surfaces, leaders need to do two things. First, they need to welcome the paradox as a challenge to see more of their current organizational reality. All leaders have blind spots. As savvy as they may be, leaders will never see the full reality of the organization. In fact, as discussed in previous chapters, leaders' views of reality are just as subjective as their colleagues'. Paradoxes provide an opportunity for leaders to expand their view of reality and fill in more bits of the big picture. A more complete picture puts them in a better position to effectively lead the organization.

Contemplating these apparent contradictions is likely to also create synergy and spark momentum. One study of the milestone contributions of fifty-eight scientists and artists, including Einstein, Picasso, and Mozart, found that their creative breakthroughs shared a common pattern. All occurred when two or more opposites were existing side by side, resulting in synergy that produced ideas never imagined in the past. Comparable visions for tomorrow's leaders could spark comparable breakthroughs as they discover their own hot fudge sundaes.

Confronting the Tension Point of Stability Versus Instability

The central challenge of leading in the midst of paradox is confrontation: embracing challenges to conventional ways of resolving the tension of the paradox. The desire for stability can lure leaders into choosing one piece of reality over another. In this short-sighted effort to remove the tension, they may unwittingly elevate tension stored inside the paradox.

To illustrate the point, consider the tension bound into the paradox of maintaining long-term organizational stability in a world of instability. Conventional wisdom tells leaders they can't have stability and instability at the same time. Either they do everything they can to stabilize their corner of the world or they confess that they are living in a world where no one is in control. Agreeing to do the former, leaders devote their precious energy to controlling, directing, and containing the forces that bombard them in unpredictable ways. In short, they resort to a lot of bossing. Eventually, sapped of energy, they grudgingly admit that their control was just an illusion. At best, they were holding the lid on the pressure cooker a little longer, feeling the pressure gradually build.

If, on the other hand, leaders acknowledge that no one is in control, they may resort to protecting their own territory from hostile takeover. The long-term effect of this approach is equally dysfunctional to leaders and the organization. Energy is spent surviving rather than thriving.

Suppose, for instance, looming budget cuts pit our department against other departments in the organization. In addition, the supervisors apparently have lost all control in sorting through this mess in a rational way. Politics determine the winners and losers. We end up doing whatever is necessary to strengthen our position and weaken our opponents'.

As repeatedly emphasized throughout this book, tomorrow's leaders have another choice when confronting paradox: They can link apparent contradictions with "and" logic. Tomorrow's leaders will ask, "How can we maintain stability and acknowledge the reality of instability around us?" The knee-jerk response will be, "We can't!" And the leaders will reply, "But if we could, how would we do it?" Herein lies the fundamental hope and optimism for those leaders who still have a fire in their belly. They will first have to acknowledge that the external world is laden with unpredictability and instability. Tomorrow's leaders simply cannot predict with confidence what specific steps will be needed to assure productivity and success. They can, however, assure their organization that people will be productive and fulfilled by relying on the internal stability of the core values they treasure most. As indicated previously, all organisms, including systems, seek stability. Otherwise, they move at the mercy of extraneous forces, without direction or integrity. Core values anchor the organization, giving it a stability that allows tomorrow's leaders to help people process constant change and proceed toward their vision, even in the face of an unstable and complex external environment.

For an organization intent on defining its own future, confronting the tension embodied in paradox is liberating, not debilitating. Positive, creative energy flows from inclusive ("and") thinking, whereas negative energy spews from exclusive (either/or) thinking. Granted, confronting the paradox can be painful, but it is also fulfilling.

TACKLING THE TENSIONS OF CONTROL VERSUS FREEDOM

In today's organization, control stems from a person's position in the hierarchy. People at the top set the expectations, the criteria for reward and recognition, and the rules determining winners and losers. As controlling messages pass downward through the organization, the unspoken assumption is that people do what they are told to do by the higher-ups. Since control supposedly shapes behavior, the bosses reward those whose actions reflect the orders of the higher-ups. This type of organizational structure breeds dependency and encourages energy to be spent in one's perceived self-interest. A person whose dominant interest is fast-track advancement will do whatever it takes in today's organization to please those at the top of the hierarchy.

The opposite of control is freedom. Loosely translated by today's leaders, freedom means organized anarchy. Left to their own devices, say today's leaders, employees act in their own selfish interest while the organization takes a distant second place. Giving employees freedom is impossible, for they would abuse it. It is an all or nothing decision for the leaders: Which will it be, centralized control or employee freedom? Inclusive thinking shifts the emphasis altogether. Instead of debating either/or choices, tomorrow's leaders will ask, "How can we maintain organizational control *and* support employee freedom?

Tomorrow's leaders will realize the power of employee freedom unencumbered by rigid hierarchies but bound by core values that control how they choose along the way. How exciting for employees in tomorrow's organization to know they will be able to live in a world of constant change and move toward their collective vision, secure in what they stand for and dream of.

With a clear, compelling vision driven by strong organizational values, individuals in tomorrow's organization are free to take risks and make mistakes. Employees can win by losing. They can advance the vision by failing and quickly learning from their discovery that they failed. In other words, adaptability to circumstances engenders control because people make midcourse corrections on their way to the overall vision for the organization. Being right isn't celebrated. Being adaptable is.

RESOLVING THE TENSION OF TEAM VERSUS INDIVIDUAL CONTRIBUTIONS

Historically, organizations have faced the dilemma of designing management structures around team productivity or individual productivity. Prevailing management thought today supports the following ways of resolving the paradox. Either we organize to support individual performance or we organize to support a team concept. If we land on the side of the equation favoring the individual, we structure reward and recognition accordingly: group cooperation gets a thumbs-down and individual stars get to climb up. If we organize by teams, the reverse is true: individuals lose their identity as teams become the focus of attention. Either way, we lose something in the process.

Tomorrow's leaders will apply "and" logic by asking, "How can we capitalize on the team concept *and* recognize the importance of individual contributions? The answer will be found by understanding the dynamics of synergy. Truly effective groups produce far more than the sum of individual contributions. The team believes the richest sources of ideas come from collectively building on individual perspectives, even the way-out ones. This is another example of the core value of *diversity* in action. Interdependency fosters group and individual value. In tomorrow's organization, each person assumes the role of creative contributor and, paradoxically, as the group becomes more important, the individual becomes more important too.

As detailed in the above examples, paradoxes will be inevitable challenges for tomorrow's leaders. But tomorrow's leaders will be well prepared to meet them. By applying inclusive thinking, both leaders and followers will find that the energy resulting from the tension of paradox can prove to be a valuable asset in discovering creative solutions to complex organizational problems.

LEADING WITH CONFIDENCE

Many leaders today will be the first to admit that leading isn't what it used to be. Fondly recalling the good old days when the pace was slower, the competition was weaker, and the profit margins were greater, people sitting at the top of the chart aren't necessarily feeling on top of many things. Whether real or perceived, the burden on leaders today seems heavier, perhaps because so many leaders are still operating under the Great Person Theory, which says that leadership means stepping forward, grabbing the reins, and taking charge.

In tomorrow's organization, leadership means assuming responsibility for influencing others. It will be more fluid and sometimes more transitory. And it clearly will be shared by many through the course of events. Tomorrow, one person sitting at the top of the chart or at the head of the table won't carry the weight of leading alone.

Knowing that things won't be easy, tomorrow's leaders nevertheless will proceed with the confidence that comes from knowing they have a set of principles and a base of knowledge that will carry them and their organization through the tough times.

Who will tomorrow's leaders be? They will be many people at various levels in the organization, not just people with certain job titles. Indeed, they will probably include you, especially if you have a mind that relishes complexity, a heart that is passionately value-driven, a soul that is destined to be keeper of the vision, and a fire that will never die! The passion and confidence of tomorrow's leaders will move us beyond what is and what has been into visions of what can be, what could be, and what has not yet been imagined.

APPENDIX A

ORGANIZATIONAL VALUES OF THE APPLETON AREA SCHOOL DISTRICT

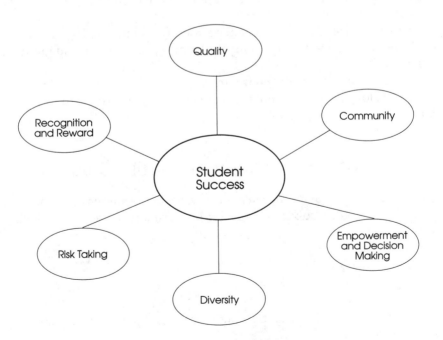

CORE ORGANIZATIONAL VALUE: STUDENT SUCCESS

The Appleton Area School District is passionately committed to student success. Student success means that each student demonstrates productivity in meaningful school work that has personal and societal value.

GUIDELINES FOR DECISION MAKING

We will:

- Inspire students to be lifelong learners in a vastly changing world.
- Bridge the world of the student, the world of the school, and the world outside the school.
- Emphasize exploration and discovery as integral to each student's school experience.
- Create an environment where students are active and interactive learners.
- Develop critical thinking, creative thinking, and problem solving.
- Provide for each student's individual development.
- Convey to each student, "You are important, you can succeed, and we will not give up on you."
- Expect all students to develop a strong work ethic.
- Measure student productivity with appropriate formal and informal assessments.
- Provide a safe, caring environment.
- Develop curriculum and instructional strategies to meet these guidelines.

SUPPORTING ORGANIZATIONAL VALUE: QUALITY

Quality instruction and other related services to the students, employees, parents, and other publics should be our primary focus for achieving student success.

GUIDELINES FOR DECISION MAKING

We will:

- Provide the necessary training to support quality instruction and other related services.

- Eliminate barriers that prevent the delivery of quality instruction and other related services.
- Provide incentives and opportunities for the continued professional growth and development of all employees.
- Provide necessary instructional materials, equipment, and personnel to support all Board-approved programs.
- Follow recruitment, selection, and evaluation practices to employ and retain the highest quality staff.
- Support and enhance the quality of the work life of all employees by providing clean, safe, and inviting facilities.
- Provide all students with equitable programs, facilities, and educational opportunities.
- Expect ongoing quality improvement in service within our district and to our other publics.

SUPPORTING ORGANIZATIONAL VALUE: EMPOWERMENT AND DECISION MAKING

The power to make decisions and effect change should be distributed throughout the organizational structure of the district by providing the necessary support, information, and resources. Participatory decision making should be integral to the effective functioning of our school district.

GUIDELINES FOR DECISION MAKING

We will:

- Involve employees who have expertise and/or interest in decisions that are relevant to them (e.g., staffing, budgeting, curriculum, materials selection, and staff development).
- Involve students, parents, and community representatives in the decision-making process.
- Design organizational structures that encourage multiple points of view and interaction beyond the typical departmental or school boundaries.
- Seek, identify, and apply pertinent research regarding district decisions.
- Train employees for leadership roles in the decision-making process.

• Keep publics informed on an ongoing basis during the decision-making process.

• Encourage decisions to be made as close to the point of implementation as possible with consideration being given to those accountable for that decision.

• Recognize that individual employees must determine how they will prioritize commitments to best achieve both individual and organizational goals.

Supporting Organizational Value: Risk Taking

Risk taking and innovation should be supported as a way of achieving organizational improvement.

Guidelines for Decision Making

We will:

• Encourage individuals and groups throughout the organization to initiate risk taking, innovation, and experimentation.

• Create an atmosphere where people can make and acknowledge mistakes without fear of "failure."

• Recognize individuals or groups for taking risks to further the mission of the district.

• Recognize that short-term setbacks may in turn result in long-term personal and/or organizational growth.

• Expect and support evaluation of experimental and innovative practices and encourage wider implementation of successful programs.

• Encourage the sharing of results from experimental or innovative practices and programs, whether they are successful or not.

• Consider conflict a sign of a healthy organization and resolve conflict in a spirit of fairness, respect, and trust.

• Encourage individuals with appropriate expertise to consider new assignments, even though these assignments may differ from past career paths.

Supporting Organizational Value: Diversity

Diversity should be valued and evident in our school district.

Guidelines for Decision Making

We will:

- Acknowledge that each student is a unique individual and provide an appropriate educational program.
- Actively implement the concept of Equal Opportunity Employment.
- Respect individuality among staff.
- Seek to maximize the strengths of diverse styles and strategies within a common district direction.
- Actively seek diverse viewpoints as a rich source of helping us see reality more fully and helping us dream more creatively.
- Expect each school/department to develop its own sense of community.
- Encourage individuals to share their expertise outside their specific job descriptions.
- Accord to all persons dignity, respect, and worth.

Supporting Organizational Value: Recognition and Reward

The accomplishments of employees should be valued and recognized in order to improve the quality of instruction and related services of our district.

Guidelines for Decision Making

We will:

- Promote peer recognition of quality instruction and related services.
- Implement a systematic, streamlined process for increasing awareness and pride in the many accomplishments of our district.
- Use a representative group of all employees when designing a creative recognition program.

• Recognize employees for excellence as a way to thank those employees and to encourage others to unlock or renew their potential for creativity, motivation, and involvement.

• Create a climate where intrinsic rewards help employees feel a sense of accomplishment.

• Make recognition public and timely, and monitor the success of the program.

SUPPORTING ORGANIZATIONAL VALUE: COMMUNITY

The district should develop and nurture a sense of community among all members. Community means that all individuals working together share a commitment to understand and honor differing perceptions and concerns as they move toward common goals in an environment of trust.

GUIDELINES FOR DECISION MAKING

We will:

• Provide an atmosphere in which nonjudgmental listening and the opportunity to express opinions freely are encouraged.

• Encourage shared problem solving at all levels.

• Remove barriers to communication among all employee groups.

• Invite frequent and active involvement in district issues from the community, parents, businesses, students, and employees.

• Provide an environment that enables the individual to work in a professionally effective and personally healthy manner.

• Acknowledge the existence of conflict and recognize that such conflict can be healthy if we actively seek resolution.

• Continue to keep visible the feeling that "we're all in this business together."

EXAMPLES OF CORE VALUES AND GUIDELINES FOR DECISION MAKING

S pecific core values will vary according to the nature of the organization or the units within the organization. The following examples, however, illustrate the general nature of core values and the questions you should ask when developing both a value and the accompanying guidelines for decision making.

CORE VALUE: EMPOWERMENT

To what extent does the district:

• value empowering employees throughout the district to assist in achieving the mission of the school district?

• value equal access by all employees to support information and resources?

• value all employees as equally important members of the organization?

CORE VALUE: DECISION MAKING

To what extent does the district:

- value placing decision making as close to the point of implementation as possible?
- value the opportunity for input in districtwide decisions?
- value decisions being made by those who are directly affected by them?

CORE VALUE: BELONGING

To what extent does the district:

- value commitment to the development of the individual within the district?
- value treating all individuals as significant stakeholders in the organization?
- value a "we" spirit and feeling of ownership in the organization?

CORE VALUE: TRUST AND CONFIDENCE

To what extent does the district:

- believe that employees act in the best interest of students and the organization?
- value employees as having the expertise to make wise decisions?
- value investing in the development of employees?

CORE VALUE: DIVERSITY

To what extent does the district:

- value differences in individual philosophy and practices?
- value differences in perspectives?
- value schools and the children within them celebrating their distinct character?

CORE VALUE: INTEGRITY

To what extent does the district:
- value honesty in words and actions?
- value consistent, responsible pursuit of what we stand for?
- value the unwavering commitment to ethical conduct?

CORE VALUE: STUDENT SUCCESS

To what extent does the district:

- value students as inherently curious learners?
- value doing whatever it takes to achieve student success?
- value students being meaningfully engaged in work that has personal value to them.

Tools for

Reaching Group

Decisions

Special thanks go to the following District Facilitators for helping compile and develop these tools: Lou Chicquette, Linda Dawson, and Martha Howard.

Nominal Group Process

Purpose: Use to gather and rank various solutions to a problem.

Time Needed: approximately 45 minutes

Procedure:

1. Begin with a clear written statement of the problem to be addressed.

2. Ask each person to spend about ten minutes writing ideas and responses on cards or a worksheet.

3. Form groups of ten or fewer and have everyone report out, round robin, each person giving one idea. Write each idea on a chart. Continue taking turns until all ideas are up. Ideas may be clarified as you go, or clarified when all ideas are charted. Clarification is aimed at making the ideas understandable, not changing or eliminating them.

4. Then ask participants in the group to list on cards the best four, five, or six ideas (whatever number seems to produce a suitable range). These ideas are then listed on a separate chart.

5. These may be further ranked by having individuals give each of them a rating of 1 to 5, with the ratings totaled for each item.

FIST TO FIVE

Purpose: Use to poll the group's feelings at any point in a discussion.

Time Needed: approximately 3 to 5 minutes

Procedure:

When asked to show a fist to five, participants show:

- Fist—Absolutely not, or disagree
- Three fingers—Neutral
- Five Fingers—Total Agreement

BRAINSTORMING

Purpose: Use to generate numerous ideas in a short period of time.

Time Needed: Approximately 15 minutes

Rules for Brainstorming:

- No criticism allowed.
- No explanations needed.
- Be freewheeling; anything goes.
- Seek combinations and improvements.
- Seek quantity over quality.
- Be spontaneous; don't respond in any predetermined order.

SORTING

Purpose: Use to narrow brainstormed lists to a workable number of ideas.

Time Needed: approximately 10 minutes

Procedure:

1. After brainstorming ways to accomplish a specific goal, post three large sheets of chart paper.
2. Ask the group to "sort" the ideas into three categories:

   - "Quick Fixes" (those ideas that are important, but can be accomplished quickly or by one individual);
   - "Out of Our Hands" (ideas that are not realistic given our present circumstances);
   - "Definite Possibilities" (the rest of the ideas).

3. Concentrate future team efforts on the "Definite Possibilities" list. Eliminate the "Out of Our Hands" list, but don't ignore the ideas in the "Quick Fix" list, for they may be the source of early and easy successes. Individual volunteers may tackle those issues, freeing the group to address more complex ideas.

CLUSTERING

Purpose: Use to merge small-group ideas into a total group product.

Time Needed: approximately 40 minutes

Procedure:

1. Ask small groups to brainstorm the solution to a problem or to generate goals on slips of paper (8½" X 11" paper cut lengthwise works nicely, as do large Post-It notes). Each brainstormed idea should be written on a separate slip.
2. After the small groups have completed brainstorming, ask one group to post one of their ideas on the wall. Ask other groups if they have any similar ideas and tape those slips directly beneath the first.
3. Ask a second group to post another idea on the wall and again ask other groups to put similar ideas beneath this one. Continue categorizing the slips in this manner until all ideas are posted.

4. Review the columns of ideas with the group and then ask them to label each of the categories. (The label should capture the essence of each cluster). Proceed with some type of ranking procedure, such as a variation of the *Nominal Group Process* or *Spend a Buck.*

SPEND A BUCK

Purpose: Use to provide a ranking system.

Time Needed: approximately 15 minutes

Procedure:

1. Distribute 3" X 5" cards to participants and ask them to write each predetermined issue or category on a card. Each participant will need as many cards as there are issues.

2. When they have finished, inform them that they have one dollar to spend. Their task is to determine which idea or ideas are most important and then divide their money accordingly. Participants write on each card how much they are willing to spend on that item.

3. Remind participants that no one can spend more than a dollar.

4. Collect the cards and tabulate.

THE 1-3-6 TECHNIQUE

Purpose: Use to obtain information when group members are reluctant to speak or when some group members tend to dominate This is an easy and fair way to prioritize issues in a relatively short time.

Time Needed: approximately 35 minutes

Procedure:

1. State the topic and allow two to three minutes for each person to list one or two ideas concerning the topic on a card.

2. Form the participants into groups of three (either voluntary or assigned groups). The groups of three discuss the ideas of each person in the group and select one or two ideas that the group can support. This usually takes seven to ten minutes.

3. Once each group has selected their priorities, they should join another group to form a group of six. Again, the goal is to discuss the choices and choose the best one or two items to represent this group of six.

4. Ideas from the groups of six are charted for everyone to see. Every person is given five sticker dots and must choose what he or she believes are the best alternatives. All five dots cannot be put on one alternative; they must be divided in some way among the alternatives. The results are graphic and apparent to all.

THE FISH BOWL

Purpose: Use to discuss the ideas generated in small groups in a large-group setting.

Time Needed: time depends on topic discussed; usually 30 to 60 minutes

Procedure:

1. Form a circle of chairs in the middle of the room (one chair per group plus one additional chair).

2. Ask each small group to elect a spokesperson who they believe will adequately express their opinions and sentiments. These spokespersons sit in the chairs in the circle.

3. The persons in the circle of chairs participate in the discussion or negotiate for a possible solution to a problem. The remainder of the participants observe and are not allowed to interject their opinions. If the observers feel that something is being overlooked, they may temporarily sit in the empty chair and participate in the discussion. Once they have made their point, however, they must return to the outside circle to free the empty chair.

SILENT CONSENSUS

Purpose: Use this as a way to help a group begin planning projects or goals.

Time Needed: approximately 1 to 1½ hours

Procedure:

1. Establish a clear question that will generate diverse responses.

2. Brainstorm responses and record all ideas on Post-It notes or cards (follow hints for brainstorming).

3. Randomly place the Post-It notes or cards on chart paper, a blackboard, a tabletop, or other flat surface.

4. Push for breakthrough thinking, then end verbal brainstorming.

5. Ask participants to *silently* sort random ideas into categories by placing like ideas in the same area.

6. Participants continue moving and removing Post-It notes or cards.

7. Consensus is reached when no one moves any more Post-It notes or cards.

8. Ask participants to develop a category statement that describes the essence of the ideas in each category, and place this statement at the top of each category, as shown in the diagram below.

9. Ask participants to prioritize categories using common sense or other prioritization tools.

Results of Silent Consensus

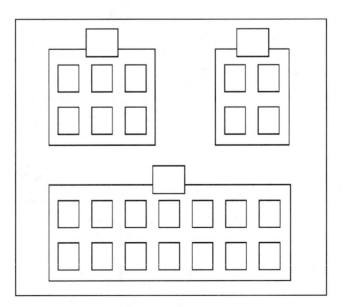

A TREE DIAGRAM

Purpose: To help move goals to implementation

Time Needed: 1 to 1½ hours

Procedure:

1. Place a goal statement to the extreme left center of a piece of chart paper.
2. Ask the group, "What target objectives do we need to meet to accomplish this goal?"
3. Write answers to this question on Post-It notes placed to the right of the goal statement (see diagram below).
4. Ask the following question of each target objective: "What activities, projects, processes need to be accomplished to achieve this target objective?"
5. Write answers to this question on Post-It notes placed to the right of each target objective (see diagram).
6. Assign each of the activities, projects, and processes generated to a person who will assume responsibility for completing the task.
7. Time lines for completion can also be added.

A Tree Diagram

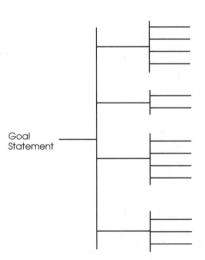

BIBLIOGRAPHY

Bergman, A.B. (1992). "Lessons for Principals from Site-Based Management." *Educational Leadership* 50, 1: 48–51.

Block, P. (1987). *The Empowered Manager: Positive Political Skills at Work*. San Francisco: Jossey-Bass.

Covey, S.R. (1990). *Principle-Centered Leadership*. New York: Summit Books.

Crum, T.F. (1987). *The Magic of Conflict*. New York: Simon and Schuster.

Fisher, R., and S. Brown. (1988). *Getting Together: Building a Relationship That Gets to YES*. Boston: Houghton Mifflin.

Fullan, M. (1991). *The New Meaning of Educational Change*. New York: Teachers College Press.

Fullan, M., and A. Hargreaves. (1991). *What's Worth Fighting For: Working Together for Your School*. Toronto: Ontario Public School Teachers' Federation.

Glickman, C.D. (May 1991). "Pretending Not to Know What We Know." *Educational Leadership* 48, 8: 4–10.

Handy, C. (1989). *The Age of Unreason*. Boston: Harvard Business School Press.

Heitmuller, P., et al. (1993). "Dimensions of Professional Growth for Educational Leaders." *Journal of Staff Development* 14, 1: 28–31.

Land, G., and B. Jarman. (1992). *Breakpoint and Beyond: Mastering the Future—Today*. New York: Harper Business.

Oakley, E., and D. Krug. (1992). *Enlightened Leadership*. Denver: Stone Tree Publishing.

Patterson, J.L., S.C. Purkey, and J.V. Parker. (1986). *Productive School Systems for a Nonrational World*. Alexandria, Va.: Association for Supervision and Curriculum Development.

Rosow, J.M., and R. Zager. (1989). *Allies in Education Reform: How Teachers, Unions, and Administrators Can Join Forces for Better Schools*. San Francisco: Jossey-Bass.

Rost, J.C. (1991). *Leadership for the Twenty-First Century*. New York: Praeger.

Sarason, S. (1990). *The Predictable Failure of Educational Reform*. San Francisco: Jossey-Bass.

Schlechty, P.C. (1991). *Schools for the Twenty-First Century: Leadership Imperatives for Educational Reform*. San Francisco: Jossey-Bass.

Seller, W. (1993). "New Images for the Principal's Role in Professional Development." *Journal of Staff Development* 14, 1: 22–26.

Senge, P.M. (1990). *The Fifth Discipline: The Art and Practice of the Learning Organization*. New York: Doubleday.

Sergiovanni, T.J. (1992). *Moral Leadership: Getting to the Heart of School Improvement*. San Francisco: Jossey-Bass.

Tichy, N.M., and M.A. Devanna. (1986). *The Transformational Leader*. New York: John Wiley and Sons.

"Transforming Leadership" [Theme issue]. (February 1992). *Educational Leadership* 49, 5.

ABOUT THE AUTHOR

J erry L. Patterson is Superintendent of Schools for the Appleton Area School District in Appleton, Wisconsin. He has more than twenty-five years' experience in public education, spanning the elementary, secondary, and university levels. He has facilitated groups and conducted workshops throughout the United States focusing on the themes in this book: leadership, core values, consensus building, group decision making, systems thinking, and conflict resolution. He may be contacted at P.O. Box 2019, Appleton, Wisconsin, 54913, or by phone at (414) 832-6126.

CURRENT ASCD

NETWORKS

A SCD sponsors numerous networks that help members exchange ideas, share common interests, identify and solve problems, grow professionally, and establish collegial relationships. The following networks may be of particular interest to readers of this book:

High Schools Networking for Change
Contact: Gil James, Principal, Sprague High School, 2373 Kuebler Rd. South, Salem, OR 97302-9404 TEL (503) 399-3261 FAX (503) 399-3407

Instructional Supervision
Contact: J. McClain Smith, Coordinator, University Programs, Hilliard City Schools, 5323 Cemetery Rd., Hilliard OH 43026 TEL (614) 771-4273 FAX (614) 777-2424

Learning Community
Contact: F. James Clatworthy, School of Education, Oakland University, Rochester, MI 48309-4401 TEL (313) 370-3052 FAX (313) 370-4202

Mentoring Leadership and Resources
Contact: Richard Lange, Director of Staff Development, Prospect Heights Public Schools, 834 Inverrary Ln., Deerfield, IL 60015 TEL (708) 870-3857 FAX (708) 870-3896

Network for Restructured Schools
Contact: Richard Ackerman and Chuck Christensen, Center for Field Service and Studies, University of Massachusetts–Lowell, One University Ave., Lowell, MA 01854 TEL (508) 934-4633 FAX (508) 934-3002

Quality Schools/OBE
Contact: Rick Scott, Chetwynd Secondary School, School District #59, P.O. Box 447, Chetwynd, B.C., Canada, VOC 1JO TEL (604) 788-2267 FAX (604) 788-9729

Staff Development
Contact: Vern Minor, Ponca ISD 613 E. Grand, Ponca, OK 74601 TEL (405) 767-8000

Strategic Planning Network: From Vision to Reality
Contact: Patricia R. Stelwagon, Principal Strategic Planning, Berryessa Union School District, 1376 Piedmont Rd., San Jose, CA 95132-2498 TEL (408) 923-1831 FAX (408) 259-3869

Teacher Leadership
Contact: Ronnie Konner, West Essex Regional School District, West Greenbrook Rd., N. Caldwell, NJ 07006 TEL (201) 228-1200 FAX (201) 575-7847

TQM—Education
Contact: John Jay Bonstingl, Consultant in Quality Education, P.O. Box 810, Columbia, MD 21044 TEL (410) 997-7555 FAX (410) 997-7555

Understanding Educational Change
Contact: Michele Keenan, 407 Enos Place, Ho-Ho-Kus, NJ 07423 TEL (201) 612-0950 FAX (201) 670-3833